MORRIS AUTOMATED INFORMATION NETWORK

W9-BGS-160

MAY 08 2018

Treating Separation Anxiety in Dogs

Malena DeMartini-P

Business Section in Chapt
by Gina Phairas of

Chester
Library

DISCARD

250 West Main Street
Chester, NJ 07930

Dogwise Publishing
Wenatchee, Washington U.S.A.

Treating Separation Anxiety in Dogs
Malena DeMartini-Price, CTC

Dogwise Publishing
A Division of Direct Book Service, Inc.
403 South Mission Street, Wenatchee, Washington 98801
1-509-663-9115, 1-800-776-2665
www.dogwisepublishing.com / info@dogwisepublishing.com

© 2014 Malena DeMartini-Price
Photos: Mary Brusco, Malena DeMartini-Price, Scout Design, Nancy Dubois, Amanda C. Fried, Amanda Hessel, Stephen Holt, Elaine Iandoli, Maria Karunungan, Eunice Lee, Blair Maus, Stephanie Pedersen, Gina Phairas, Kevin M. Price, Ken Rich, Dorit Ron, Jessica Rollins, Eveline Shen, Swanson Vitamins
Graphic design: Lindsay Peternell
Cover design: Brittney Kind

All rights reserved. No part of this book may be reproduced or transmitted in any form or by any means, electronic, digital or mechanical, including photocopying, recording or by any information storage or retrieval system without permission in writing from the publisher.

Limits of Liability and Disclaimer of Warranty:
The author and publisher shall not be liable in the event of incidental or consequential damages in connection with, or arising out of, the furnishing, performance, or use of the instructions and suggestions contained in this book.

Library of Congress Cataloging-in-Publication Data
DeMartini-Price, Malena, 1968-
  Treating separation anxiety in dogs / by Malena DeMartini-Price, CTC ; business section in chapter 15 written by Gina Phairas of Dog-tec.
    pages cm
  Includes index.
  ISBN 978-1-61781-143-2
  1. Dogs--Psychology. 2. Dogs--Behavior. I. Phairas, Gina. II. Title.
  SF433.D46 2014
  636.7--dc23
                                    2014006725

ISBN: 978-1-61781-143-2

Printed in the U.S.A.

Dedication

I dedicate this book to every owner of a
dog who suffers from separation anxiety. I
understand and empathize with your plight
and I want you to know you are not alone.
There is hope. Be strong, have faith, celebrate
the small victories, and don't give up.

Table of Contents

Acknowledgements

This book wouldn't be a reality if it weren't for a few stellar individuals that have contributed in their own unique ways. There are many others who I hold dear and am grateful to as well, but these people deserve a special mention.

First of all I owe sincere gratitude to Jean Donaldson whose amazing tutelage has allowed me to have the science based behavior career that I have today. Wow, 13 years and counting and I am still learning from you.

Special thanks to Rikke Jorgenson whose guidance through the writing process of this book made me a better writer and communicator, and in many ways a better person. It makes me so happy to now call her my friend.

Particular thanks to Janis Bradley who took great care to review my early manuscript and give feedback without which I would not have realized that I was omitting such important information. Thank you.

And of course the business section in this book I believe is an integral part for which I am ever so grateful to Gina Phairas for contributing. Thank you Gina for all of your brilliant wisdom and for joining me in our seminars—you are amazing!

What can I possibly say as words of gratitude to Sandi Thompson who has written the foreword to this book. It was a terrific journey with Sam, and I am so glad I was a part of it and that the two of you are thriving now. Thank you for the gift of your words.

I have a unique place in my heart for my wonderful clients. You have all been gracious enough to trust me with your precious dogs' behavior and the difficult, often emotional ride that you face with this disorder. I am honored to have been the one to guide you through this process.

I can't say enough about the remarkable team at Dogwise Publishing. You have all been so terrific from the moment you took on this manuscript from such a novice as myself. Thank you for walking me through this process with such kindness.

Finally, but not at all in the least, I owe a loving tribute to my adoring husband Kevin. He honestly takes care of me in every way (seriously, like including laundry and everything) so that I can tuck my head into my computer and care for my clients for hours and hours a day. When I started to become so busy that we didn't have time for date nights anymore he just said he loved me and told me he was proud of how many people and dogs I was helping. How lucky I am to be so loved. Thank you Kevin with all of my heart, we'll have date nights again soon—I promise.

Foreword

by Sandi Thompson, CPDT-KA

Siam Sam was a scrawny street dog living in Thailand during "The Great Bangkok Flood of 2011." He and two other dogs were found on the second floor of an abandoned building seeking refuge from rising flood waters. The province had been declared a disaster zone, all the local people evacuated. The already ten-foot water levels were rising daily. Hundreds, perhaps thousands, of animals had died and the survivors were facing death by drowning, starvation and disease. But this was Sam's lucky day: he and his two dog friends were spotted peering out the second story window by an animal rescue team patrolling the streets by boat.

Sam and friends were lured to the boat with food, sedated and then transported to a makeshift shelter at a cattle facility. There were hundreds of dogs there whom I was helping to house and care for while waiting for the water to recede so they could be returned to the streets. It was here in this crude shelter that Sam and I met.

When I brought Sam home from Thailand, I discovered that he had that disorder I had studiously avoided my whole career—separation anxiety—and he had it in a severe form. He screamed hysterically, panted frantically, clawed at doors, evacuated his bowels and chewed his forelegs bloody within minutes of being left alone. I was heartbroken. I had anticipated he might have a hard time adjusting to his new life and that it would take patience, time, and understanding. I also knew that, considering the trauma he'd been through, there was a chance he would suffer from *some* separation anxiety, and was completely on board for that.

But I wasn't prepared for the severity of his disorder, and I wasn't prepared for the hardship of helping him overcome his affliction.

Before Sam, I could not imagine going through the tedious protocol involved and not being able to leave my house during the lengthy rehab process. You see, this is why I never took on sep-anx cases. If I couldn't picture myself spending hours each week doing mindlessly dull, repetitive desensitizing departure drills with the dog's success measured in seconds, how could I advise someone else to do it?

And I wasn't alone. The secret sentiment among my trainer peers was that we'd rather have any other behavior problem with our own dogs than separation anxiety. Well, the joke was now on me. While I had been a professional reward-based dog trainer for nearly 30 years in the San Francisco Bay Area, I've never shied away from behavior challenges, with one exception: separation anxiety. Luckily I had for years been referring all my "sep-anx" cases to Malena DeMartini-Price, the only trainer in the area that would take them on, stick with them for the long haul and actually solve them. In fact, Malena worked exclusively with SA and had hundreds of successful outcomes.

So while I was daunted by Sam's severe problem, Malena was able to guide me through the process step by step. She gently coached me, reassured me when my spirits were down and expertly got me through it. It took eight months. It was hard, but not impossible. Now, Sam is completely relaxed while home alone and I joke that he eagerly pushes me out the door in order to be granted his special "alone-time Kong." A complete 180.

Treating Separation Anxiety in Dogs will give trainers systematic instruction in as well as the confidence to work with separation anxiety. We very much need a well-armed body of sep-anx schooled trainers. Dog training is currently unlicensed, unregulated, and without consumer protection or educational requirements, so owners of sep-anx dogs too often fall victim to snake-oil salesmen wielding not just useless but often harmful advice.

I shudder to think of the amazing dogs like Sam who never get the help they deserve because good trainers shy away from this problem, as I once did. Dogs with separation anxiety needn't live in misery or be euthanized because there are not enough educated trainers to skillfully guide people through their treatment.

This exciting book is a long time coming. It is the most important dog training book in decades. It will help save countless dogs. It will radically change the number of trainers solving separation anxiety cases. Read it. Use it. Be part of this change.

Introduction:
The Separation Anxiety
Treatment Myth

A myth exists among trainers, veterinarians, behaviorists and dog owners that separation anxiety is close to impossible to treat. And yet I know from experience—and from mounds of research—that separation anxiety is highly treatable. In fact, in my experience, about three out of four dogs can be fully relieved from their suffering, an astounding percentage in the realm of canine disorders.

Why, then, is the myth so widespread and persistent?

Mainly because the process of treating separation anxiety is slow— sometimes excruciatingly so—and often badly carried out. Many owners give up on separation anxiety training in the early frustrating stages when it looks as though no progress is being made on the mistaken assumption that their dog's case is one of the untreatable ones. And so the myth grows.

In this book, you will learn how to make separation anxiety treatment work by observing the dog's behaviors and body language to establish the proper course of treatment. Using management strategies, technology and medications when appropriate, you will tailor a training and behavior modification plan to meet the needs of separation anxiety dogs, and you will also learn how to teach the dog's owner to carry out the treatment protocol you recommend. Lastly you will learn how to make treating separation anxiety a viable part of your professional training business.

Separation anxiety affects about 17% of the 78 million dogs in the United States (according to Eli Lily, a drug company), a staggering number by any standards. These unfortunate dogs and their owners need help from qualified trainers, which makes separation anxiety both a business opportunity and a chance to make a much-needed difference. It's my hope that many of the trainers who have found separation anxiety training too difficult to take on will get a new perspective on the process through this book.

This book is written for trainers and is intended for them to use as a guide to treating separation anxiety with their clients. However, I have used non-technical language so trainers can share the book with owners should they want to. I'm also convinced that owners willing to dedicate time and patience to the process can pick up this book and work on their dog's separation anxiety problem on their own. Please note that the appendices at the back of the book contain information that should not be overlooked, including client handouts, an initial consultation questionnaire and detailed training instructions for teaching key behaviors such as relax/stay and go to your mat in case you need to refer to them.

1

Treating Separation Anxiety in Dogs—An Overview

The main ingredient for successful treatment of separation anxiety is unwavering and compassionate support from a skilled trainer. Remember, owners of a separation anxiety dog will know nothing about how to overcome the problem. They have no frame of reference, no prior experience (most likely) and no behavior modification protocols to refer to. They find it inconceivable that the one- or two-minute absences you will ask them to work on could ever translate into the dog being able to cope with four-hour absences. The *gradual* process of this type of protocol is difficult for most owners and, without strong guidance from a trainer, few can stay the course successfully.

The treatment protocols I recommend are time-intensive and require the owners to make the commitment of a substantial period of time, usually several weeks, during which they are asked to not leave their dogs alone. So, for separation anxiety treatment to be successful, you must be not only patient, but willing to work closely with owners without getting frustrated with them or with the training process itself. You have to cheerlead, empathize, support and encourage your clients while finding new and creative ways to explain and approach problems to break through plateaus, as well as being able to discover and point out the incremental progress made so the owner's motivation doesn't falter. You must be hands-on with your clients, because a program like this can't simply be handed over to the owners without support. If you do, they won't succeed.

I work with my owners several days a week via phone, email and live web sessions to make sure they stay on track and to keep them motivated. I suggest you maintain this level of contact as well. But be honest with yourself. Is this is a good fit for your training skills and temperament? If not, refer separation anxiety clients to another trainer. Plenty of dogs with other issues need your help.

To guide the owners and the dog through the twists and turns of the separation anxiety treatment roadmap, the training plans I recommend are divided into phases. You won't progress to the next phase until the dog is truly successful in the previous one. This is necessitated by the sheer variety of separation anxiety displays you might come across, which means there's no cookie-cutter solution that works with all dogs. But by using the phases, you can work with all the different types of cases and reach the important benchmarks without moving too quickly. For example, if a dog can't successfully stay behind a baby gate for a few minutes while Mom is out of view (in Phase Three), you can't advance to the next phase. This ensures that you won't impede progress by moving too quickly and can keep the clients within the proper parameters.

Some key training terminology

There are a variety of terms that will be used throughout this book that many trainers will already know. However, for novice trainers or less experienced owners reading this book, I have included a few terms here that you may not be familiar with which will come up frequently during the course of the book, especially when creating a separation anxiety protocol:

Cue: A cue is a word or action that is used to communicate to a dog what you want him to do. For instance the verbal cue "Sit" informs the dog that you want him to put his bottom on the ground. The word itself has absolutely no meaning until we have trained that the cue has a behavior associated with it. Therefore you could train the cue "Banana" to mean "Stay" instead of using the word "Stay." The same concept also applies to hand signals or an action such as rattling a set of keys to let your dog know, for example, to come and sit at the door.

Threshold: We are going to be referring to a dog's threshold often. The term threshold is used in separation anxiety treatment to indicate when a dog is starting to display signs of anxiety and stress related to being left alone. It is our job in a separation anxiety protocol to watch the dog's body language carefully to keep him below his anxiety threshold. If you are able to keep him relatively calm and relaxed, his condition would be labeled **"sub-threshold."**

Criteria: In dog training, the term criteria means what the owner/trainer expects the dog to do when asked at a given time while training or modifying behavior. If, for example, you are just beginning to teach a recall to a dog, your initial criterion might be just a glance in your direction when you call him. Once he does that, you might boost your criteria to include the dog moving in your direction. When creating steps for a separation anxiety protocol, we will often refer to criteria setting, for example seeing if a dog can remain calm for 30 seconds when left alone, then 60 seconds. Setting criteria helps you to decide whether or not you are moving too fast and makes it more likely that the dog will make progress without going over threshold. You will also see that I refer to **"splits"** in criteria. This means that when the criteria you set are too difficult for the dog, you must figure out a way to split your new criteria between the level the dog could handle previously and the new level that has proven to be too hard. Dividing steps into levels of minutia is often necessary, so instead of raising your time alone criteria from 30 to 60 seconds, you might choose 45 seconds instead.

Desensitization and counter-conditioning: Much of your work with owners during the treatment phase includes desensitization and counter-conditioning. The dog needs to be desensitized to being left alone and he needs to learn that being left alone in the confinement area can actually be a pleasant experience. It is the process of desensitizing and counter-conditioning that takes such a long time in most separation anxiety cases. During desensitization the scary stimulus (being left alone in this case) is introduced at whatever level the dog can handle without producing anxiety. It is then gradually increased while keeping the dog below his anxiety threshold, always building upon success. Counterconditioning is a process where the scary stimulus (say the confinement area) is coupled with something fabulous like stuffed food toys, thereby changing the emotional response from a bad one to a terrific one.

Variable schedule: When using a desensitization protocol for separation anxiety training it is important to vary the times in which you are gone. Rather than move in a straight line where the time gets longer and longer with each repetition, it is important to vary the duration of your absences. Some absences should be shorter, some longer and some medium in length, always with the goal in mind that you are trying to increase the duration overall. Think about keeping the durations on a constantly fluctuating schedule so that the dog not only isn't getting anxious about the fact that the absences seem to be getting longer and longer each time, but also is not anticipating a pattern to the absences and does not know whether the next one will be long, short or medium in duration.

What is separation anxiety?

Separation anxiety in a dog is the equivalent of a full-blown panic attack in a human being due to the anxiety and fear of being left alone. The severity of the panic attack and the way each dog manifests and displays it may be different, but the physiological basics are the same. Fear and anxiety are best friends, and the hormonal and neuro-chemical processes that happen when these emotions are triggered are not under simple mind control, certainly not by dogs (and generally not by humans, either). We can't explain to our dogs that we will be home soon so they should just "get a grip." A house-trained dog doesn't pee on the carpet when an owner is gone because he is angry; rather, he is so panicked that he pees himself. Urination, defecation, salivation, howling, barking, destruction and self-mutilation are just some of the outward displays of this internal anxiety and fear. The symptoms are horribly inconvenient or disturbing to the owners, and may cause expensive damage, complaints by neighbors and just plain general misery. Our job as trainers or owners is not simply to stop the outward display of symptoms, but rather to treat the underlying problem.

One problem you may encounter with a new clients is that their focus is on halting the symptoms—barking, house soiling, chewing and the like. While the owners may need the barking to stop out of fear of eviction, the focus must be on stopping the anxiety to end the dog's daily suffering that leads to constant barking. The outward symptoms stop when the internal suffering ends, never the other way around. Separation anxiety is simply a fear (mind you, a big one) of being left alone. Separation anxiety can develop for many reasons, but regardless of the onset, treatment can be quite successful.

When it is and when it's not

Most trainers can easily diagnose a dog with moderate-to-severe separation anxiety. In mild cases, however, you often have to use a process of exclusion. There's a possibility the dog has been improperly house-trained, is under-stimulated and/or under-exercised or is simply too young to have unsupervised access to larger areas of the house. When something as simple as confining the dog to an area where he can't see the street diminishes his barking dramatically when left alone, the behavior has little or nothing to do with separation anxiety.

With mild-to-moderate scenarios, it can be more difficult to tell whether separation anxiety is causing the problematic behavior(s). Dogs who haven't been properly desensitized to a crate or are crate averse (for various reasons) may vocalize and paw in their crates when left alone, but may very quickly learn to be alone when left in a more open confinement area. Dogs who have a propensity for demand barking can also be tough to diagnose, particularly if they have been rewarded often for the behavior. A dog who barks to be let out of his confinement area and gets his way regularly can look very similar to a dog vocalizing from anxiety. Being able to tell the difference between demand barking and anxiety barking in these types of cases is key.

The cases most commonly misinterpreted by owners are those of the under-stimulated and/or under-exercised dog. The owner returns home to garbage strewn around the house, socks tossed about the living room along with other wreckage, and then understandably judges the debris as the evidence of separation anxiety. In reality, many of these dogs are just bored and need vigorous exercise and a proper "job" to do during absences

It can be hard to tell at first glance whether this is separation anxiety or boredom. This dog is suffering from separation anxiety with symptoms of destruction, vocalization and hyper-vigilant scanning for her owner to return.

Contributing factors

In the vast majority of separation anxiety cases I have worked on, one or more of the following contributing factors was apparent:

- Multiple instances of re-homing (or sometimes just one re-homing).

- Illness or malnutrition (particularly severe) during puppyhood.

- Singleton puppies (only one in the litter).

- Never being left alone then suddenly being left alone.

- Death of a family member (animal or human).
- Introduction of a new family member (animal or human).
- Moving to a new home/apartment.
- Change in schedules or return to work after long time off.
- Removal from litter too young.
- Air shipping in cargo particularly during puppyhood.
- A traumatic event such as a tornado or a robbery.
- Noise phobia (co-morbid with separation anxiety).
- Seizure disorders.
- Old age and/or pain-related onset.

Airline shipping in cargo during puppyhood can be a contributing factor to separation anxiety.

In the hundreds of cases I have treated, only a tiny percentage of the dogs appeared to have no contributing reason for their separation anxiety. In these rare cases there were no siblings or parents with separation anxiety or other fear disorder, they weren't singleton puppies, they weren't air shipped at a young age, weren't removed from the litter at too young an age and didn't experience any illness during early development or young puppyhood. Some dogs do appear to have a strong genetic predisposition for separation anxiety, although nobody really knows for sure. I have worked with numerous puppies who displayed separation anxiety-like traits and it's tempting to label those genetic. But even young puppies can create profound learning experiences from *perceived* trauma, so in the absence of in-depth scientific studies and hard data, who can tell? I hope to do such a study someday—or that someone else does.

In addition to the factors listed above, early or improper weaning and a variety of other early puppy raising practices can contribute greatly to separation anxiety. Therefore it's important to raise awareness of the risks involved to dog fanciers, the breeding community and among those who will be purchasing or adopting dogs. Trainers who work with puppies, for example, can do a great deal of good by helping owners prevent separation anxiety from occurring in the first place. Naturally, puppy trainers can't change history, say if a dog has already been air shipped, but they can help tremendously by having owners set the puppy up to not be coddled for weeks on end and then suddenly be left alone.

I mention this here because the length of time a dog has been experiencing separation anxiety has a bearing on the prognosis. A dog presenting with a sudden onset of separation anxiety, say after moving to a new house, will generally respond to the treatment protocol much more quickly than a five-year-old dog who was air shipped as a seven-week-old puppy and has had separation anxiety since then.

2

Diagnosing Separation Anxiety and Its Severity

In practical terms, diagnosing separation anxiety is a two-step process. Once you have ruled out such things as a house-training problem or under-stimulation/lack of exercise as the underlying cause, you need to assess the severity level of the anxiety. To gather the information you need you must discuss the dog's history with the owners (more on this later). Some typical questions might include: Is the dog anxious all the time or can he be calm when the owners are home but in another room? Will the dog eat a simple meal if the owners walk out of view? Does the dog also have severe noise phobia? You will also need to observe the dog yourself, and I recommend that you use video to get the up-close look you need for a diagnosis. I'll discuss various taping technologies later, but if newer technology isn't an option, even the simplest video camera will do to capture some of the body language and activity the dog is displaying.

Note: Many owners haven't left their dog alone for a long time because they know how bad the dog's separation anxiety is. In these cases, use your judgment about whether or not to create an absence just for the sake of baseline video documentation. If the severity level is extreme, I prefer not to, but if it's an open question, keep the absence brief, at most 30 minutes.

Let's look at diagnosis in a little more detail by reviewing the symptoms of mild, moderate and severe cases.

Mild cases

In milder cases, dogs may present with pacing, whining, intermittent barking and chewing in the absence of the owners and somewhat excessive greetings when they return. The emphasis here is on the intermittent nature of the barking or whining. The dog may whine, bark or even break into a bit of a howl for a time, but will then sleep or settle. After a time, the dog may resume vocalization again, but the fact that he is able to settle for brief periods places the dog in the mild category and bodes well for prognosis. Note also that the chewing is quite mild. Typically these dogs are not even chewing at points of entry, but rather chewing on a shoe that was left out or maybe their bedding. No feats of great destruction here, often just some nibbling on an item that carries the familiar scent of the owner. While you'll often see an excited greeting upon the owners return with these mild cases, it is nothing like more moderate to severe cases. Mild-case separation anxiety dogs may leap about and even vocalize a bit when their owners return, but the key thing to notice is how quickly the dog is able to settle back down once the owner is present. Usually it takes under a minute, or at most two, before the dog is acting normally again. Remember, even non-separation anxiety dogs can be awfully excited to see their owners returning after an absence.

An important note about mild case dogs and a distinction I would like to make clear: Most mild cases do not involve a hyper-attachment to one individual. This distinction means that the dog may be labeled as having isolation distress rather than separation anxiety. In other words, the dog can be left with any ol' warm body, rather than having to have a specific person be with him at all times.

Nibbling on shoes, familiar scent items or bedding, rather than causing major destruction at entry points when left alone, is common in mild cases.

Moderate cases

The majority of cases a trainer is likely to encounter fall into the moderate category. Many of the symptoms are different than in mild cases. The first thing I typically witness is anorexia. Moderate case dogs, when presented with tasty goodies while alone, will commonly not consume them. Having said this, anorexia does *not* have to be present in order for the dog to be considered moderate to severe. I see many separation anxiety questionnaires that ask if the dog will consume food when left alone and if that box is checked "yes," then the dog is ruled not to have separation anxiety. Don't make this mistake. Many dogs eat voraciously when left alone and still have serious levels of separation anxiety. Just consider anorexia a common symptom and note it as one that puts the dog into the moderate category.

In the moderate category, barking is usually close to constant rather than intermittent. There are few breaks in the vocalization and no times where the dog just relaxes or sleeps. Additionally, the destruction you'll see here is considerably worse, usually at points of entry and carried out with more determination. One thing of note about dogs in the moderate category is that many of the symptoms are *involuntary*. By involuntary, I mean bodily functions are not under the dog's control, such as panting, elimination and sweaty paws. You'll also see an increase in severity of some of the symptoms discussed in the mild category, such as the excessive greeting behavior. Moderate case dogs may have considerable difficulty calming down after the owners return and may display quite wildly when the owner walks through the door. This is not just the usual "happy to see you" routine, but screaming, body hurling and other shenanigans beyond the norm, possibly lasting for ten minutes or more without reprieve. Finally, you may also see shadowing/following from dogs in the moderate category. The owner can't get up to get a glass of water without the dog jolting from a deep sleep to follow, and many owners can scarcely use the restroom alone. It's not uncommon to see a bit of this in the mild cases too, but in moderate cases it's more noticeable. Note that the dog may have just one or all of the above listed symptoms to be considered moderate separation anxiety.

Severe cases

Moderate case dogs are hard enough to watch, but severe case dogs are downright painful. In this category, the first symptom to look out for is self-mutilation. You'll often see the dog licking or chewing himself, typically on the forepaws and occasionally on the rear paws or the tail tip or base. This condition, called acral lick granuloma or acral lick dermatitis, requires medical attention and is among the more serious in the realm of separation anxiety symptoms. Another severe symptom you might see is escapism. I count this as severe because dogs often do great harm to themselves in the process of trying to escape. I have seen broken teeth and nails, severe lacerations and maimed eyes. Clearly, all sorts of bodily harm can result when dogs break windows or doors, bend crates or scale fences in their attempts to escape. The destruction you'll see in these cases is significant, which not only puts fiscal hardship on the owners but is dangerous for the dogs.

The involuntary symptoms of severe case dogs are worse as well. Some dogs suffer with diarrhea to the point where they can't keep weight on and can become severely dehydrated. Severe vomiting can lead to aspirated pneumonia. You might see excessive salivation, with the dogs leaving pools of drool behind, and you may witness dramatic shedding, a phenomenon often called "blowing one's coat." The barking and howling you'll hear at this stage is truly panicked and often causes problems with neighbors or homeowner associations. By far the majority of cases in the severe category require pharmacological support.

Often in separation anxiety cases, a dog experiences anxiety due to his body producing a surge of cortisol and other stress chemicals. If the owners' absences happen regularly, the anxiety is almost constant and the chemicals remain in the body continually, preventing the dog from ever truly relaxing. In such a heightened state of fear and anxiety, it's very difficult for dogs (or humans, for that matter) to learn relaxation, and the rate of progress with these dogs is much slower if at all evident. Note that the dog may have just one or all of the above listed symptoms to be considered severe separation anxiety.

Assessing Separation Anxiety Severity

Mild	Moderate	Severe
Pacing	Anorexia	Self mutilation
Whining	Elimination	Escapism
Mild chewing (i.e. bedding)	Moderate destruction	Severe destruction
Intermittent barking	Constant barking/ howling	Salivation/drooling
Mild excessive greeting	Moderate excessive greeting	Extreme excessive greeting
Mild depression	Moderate depression	Severe depression
Some shadowing owner	Sweaty paws	Excessive shedding
No key owner attachment	Panting	Excessive water consumption
	Frequent shadowing	Diarrhea/vomiting
	Pre-departure anxiety	Aggression

Having an overview of symptoms that range from mild, moderate and severe can be useful to see the progression.

Becoming familiar with the different degrees of severity of separation anxiety allows you to set up your treatment protocol accordingly. It can also help you determine whether or not you're willing to take on a particular case—you might be comfortable working with mild and moderate cases but not the severe variety. One final important thing to note: the level of severity doesn't always mean the case will take longer to resolve. Occasionally, mild cases move along at a snail's pace with resolution taking months, while severe cases might progress at almost miraculous speed. Typically, though, progress happens as you would expect, with mild cases resolving more quickly and severe cases taking longer and being more complicated.

Destruction activity can occur quickly in severe cases. Here Norman destroyed a freshly painted door in well under an hour.

Destruction can also lead to self-harm. The dog who chewed on the door and dug at the floor bloodied her gums and nails.

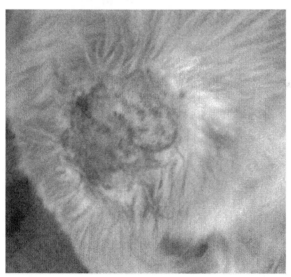

Acral lick dermatitis is a very serious symptom. The anxious dog may lick and chew on himself excessively. The self-mutilation shown here is above the tail although is often seen on the forepaws.

3

Treatment Components

As noted in the Introduction, the treatment of separation anxiety generally takes a long time, and the cooperation of the owners is needed to comply with whatever treatment plan you recommend. Since my protocol relies upon not leaving the dog alone (suspending absences) until he shows he can tolerate it, owners are likely going to have to make changes in their lives for at least a few weeks. So before you actually begin treating the dog, you must secure the *buy-in of the owners.*

A contract with the dog

There are many opinions about the treatment of separation anxiety and you can find numerous suggestions on approaches that even include leaving the untreated dog alone on a regular basis when necessary. Many trainers are really shocked when I discuss the fact that, in order to treat separation anxiety successfully, the dog must not be left alone during the treatment until such time as he is ready. Now wait, don't stop here and toss the book out just yet. Hear me out. This is really doable. I do it with my clients every day, all the time, and I will show you how to find solutions later in the book. What I am talking about here is essentially creating a contract between you, the owners and the dog. "Max, I will not leave you for longer than you can handle without getting anxious." That may be just one second on day one, but with training that one second of today will be 30 seconds by the end of the week and then a few minutes several days later and, before you know it, it is 26 minutes, then 42, then 97 and then four hours. It will be your job as the skilled professional to explain to the owner why this is so important. If you leave the dog alone to experience regular absences filled with panic, he will not be able to learn that absences are safe. In Chapter 5 you will see all of the different management tools available to help suspend absences.

Working with owners (no sugar-coating!)

Another important reason separation anxiety treatment often is ineffective is that follow-through by the owners is so poor. Often owners set out treating the disorder with great enthusiasm and work on exercises diligently for a few weeks, only to give up within the first month because they don't see the results they expect (I call this the Week 3 Blues). We trainers must accept our fair share of responsibility for this. Clearly, we need to manage our clients' expectations better. No, they won't be putting on their dancing shoes by next weekend—or in three weeks—unless they have a dog sitter.

Even a mild separation anxiety case is difficult to address if the owners have no time, patience or financial resources. The treatment program can be frustrating, particularly for those owners with little or no knowledge of training or behavior. In such cases, you can't expect them to understand the level of involvement that will be required of them. Through gentle guidance and discussion about the process, you need to assess whether they are willing and able to maintain a treatment program. While empathy and diplomacy are keys to successful consultations with distressed owners, sugar-coating the problem or the process involved is a bad idea. The treatment might take several weeks, a few months or even longer, and much will depend on both the dog's rate of learning and the owners' rate of learning and commitment level. This means you can't put a definitive time line on the resolution of the problem. But owners naturally want an answer, right now, to the question of how long it's going to take. As greatly as you may empathize with your clients—I know I do—don't fall for the temptation to guess. Too many variables are at play to do so.

Let me lay it on the line for you. Mild cases take on average six to twelve weeks to resolve and moderate-to-severe cases can take four to six months or more. I don't quote these numbers so you will spout them off to your clients—and they may not be accurate for the particular case you are working on—but so you know what kind of time commitment these cases usually demand.

An owner has to want to pursue treatment because she wants her dog to get better so both she and the dog can live happier, more peaceful lives. Wanting your dog to stop barking or destroying the furniture is legitimate, sure, but a client with a hard and fast deadline in mind is a recipe for disaster.

Time and finances are factors in another way, too. I wish this wasn't the case, but for a lot of people, it is. If an owner works 40+ hours a week and has a newborn baby, there may not be enough time to practice exercises. If an owner doesn't have the funds to use a day-care or dog walker or sitter when necessary, the dog will likely face stretches of alone time that are unacceptable for treatment. In either case, the prognosis is bleak. At the beginning of a treatment plan, one or two 30-minute sessions per day can be enough, but as the program moves forward, it's necessary to train owner absences of longer duration. To make this happen, an owner needs to have the time to train or the financial resources to pay for day training.

Obviously, your assessment of the owner's ability to work a treatment program is important. So is the need for you to explain how it can be done, to encourage the owners through the confusion of information and to support them through the emotional rollercoaster a separation anxiety treatment program can be.

And you thought you were training dogs!

How long will it take?

Of 100 owners whose dogs suffer from separation anxiety, 99 will ask the same question: How long will it take before my dog is better? An entirely reasonable question. More and more, we expect immediate results in all areas of our lives. We used to call ours a microwave society, but even that sounds archaic now with cell phones, texting, wireless Internet access and instant messaging. But our dogs run on analog as we race forward on digital. Separation anxiety training doesn't fit neatly into the fast-paced lives we have become comfortable with, it forces us to slow down and work at a pace that may seem excruciating.

Try to get your clients to embrace the process without focusing too much on the initial results. However much you might wish to, you can't predict how fast progress will happen. The only thing you can say is that getting to a better place won't happen unless the work is undertaken.

Five key treatment components

There are five key components of separation anxiety treatment, all of which will be reviewed in more detail later in this book. They are:

- Medication/Supplements (Chapter 4)
- Management (Chapter 5)
- Technology (Chapter 6)
- Toys/Games (Chapter 7)
- Training and Behavior Modification (Chapters 10-14)

For some separation anxiety dogs, you will need just one or a couple of the five components; for most, however, you'll need every single one.

Medication/Supplements: Pharmacological help can be incredibly useful with separation anxiety dogs. In some cases, dogs suffer from anxiety not just when left alone but constantly, and these dogs need help to lower their anxiety levels before they can respond to the training. We trainers, of course, neither can nor should prescribe medications, nor should we be advising clients on the topic—rather, we should be referring them to a qualified veterinarian. The section I'm including later in this book about the medications and supplements available for separation anxiety dogs is meant only as education.

Management: This is another foundational component of separation anxiety training, one that no treatment plan for separation anxiety can do without. By "management," I mean setting things up to avoid premature absences during the treatment process. In other words, if you have reached the point where you can leave the dog alone for 30 minutes, you must have someone look after the dog if you are going to need to leave for a longer period of time. Planning an absence longer than 30 minutes in this case would be premature. A dog experiencing premature absences on a regular basis won't learn to relax and will fear being alone during absences *of any length*. Such absences are called "super-threshold" absences because the dog is beyond his anxiety threshold. This must be avoided at all costs. Management options may include a crate or a baby gate in the house used during training sessions, the use of daycare or an all-day dog sitter/walker, friends or neighbors to watch over the dog and other types of coverage for absences. Whatever options you and your client end up choosing, managing a dog's anxiety level is crucial to treatment success.

Technology: It's a brave new high-tech world, and technological advancements have made treatment of separation anxiety easier and more accurate than just a decade ago. When I first started treating separation anxiety, I would lug my video camera to every client appointment and then go back to pick up the tapes at the end of the week for review so I could see how the dog was doing and set my criteria accordingly. Sometimes I would find we were accidentally pushing the dog too quickly, and other times I realized we could have pushed the dog further and had missed an opportunity to progress. Now we have webcams and smartphones and can watch the dog in real time and adjust our criteria then and there. This has dramatically expedited the treatment process. While technology use is not a must, most separation anxiety cases benefit from it. In addition, the use of webcams allows for the trainer to set up sessions with the client in order to check in frequently without having to do in-person consults. The majority of my client sessions are done online; I rarely have to meet with clients frequently in person anymore.

Toys/Games/Equipment: A whole section about toys? Definitely. Toys and games can be surprisingly effective at helping dogs with separation anxiety create positive associations with being left alone. Many clients ask about this. Given that separation anxiety dogs often won't eat or play when left alone, why use toys or food at all? Toys, games and food are most effective in the early stages when the dog is getting used to the confinement area behind a baby gate while the owner is home. An early goal is to get the dog to love the heck out of that confinement area and to build a pleasurable association between the owner hanging out with the dog in the vicinity while he enjoys his toys, games and food.

Training and Behavior Modification: Almost all separation anxiety dogs need a behavior modification plan to get better. Training will include gradual desensitization to absences and often takes considerable time and patience to implement. Absence desensitization is the foundation piece of any separation anxiety dog's improvement even though using the other four components is important as well. With some lucky dogs, you can get resolution through modest amounts of training combined with management and toys. But most need the whole enchilada.

4

Medications and Supplements

Medications and/or natural supplements can and even should be used in some cases when working with separation anxiety afflicted dogs. Not every dog with separation anxiety needs to be medicated. But in many cases, particularly more severe ones, the owners should seek veterinary counsel about medical options. I feel all owners should at least notify their veterinarian that their dog is experiencing separation anxiety and keep him or her in the loop.

Please note that in the discussion of the five phases of the separation anxiety treatment protocol that follows beginning in Chapter 10, I do not make medication and supplement recommendations. As mentioned before, that needs to be done by the owner's veterinarian. As a trainer however, you need to understand the use of the drugs and supplements and to know what your clients are getting from their veterinarians. Besides, many veterinarians want to know what type of treatment you're pursuing and aim to prescribe medication accordingly, so open communication between trainer and vet is always helpful—so in such circumstances it's good to be familiar with the basic medical options.

When to recommend contacting a vet about medication
Medication is warranted in a variety of separation anxiety cases, and while it's not your job to prescribe, you can educate your clients about medications as an option and why/when contacting their vet about

medications may be useful. Dogs who are unable to settle even when the owner is home need medication, period. If the dog exhibits anxiety-related symptoms such as excessive hyper-vigilance about even the slightest movements of family members, pacing even when the family is relaxing, whining when one family member exits the room or house, and general anxiety display at all times even when owners are present then this is a dog that cannot settle. It is in clear contrast to a normal dog's state of being when in his most comfortable state. So whether it is a hyper Border Collie or a sedentary Greyhound, what needs to be gauged is whether or not the dog can calm down completely within his breed temperament range without displaying anxiety about being left alone by his owners even when others are present. Additionally, dogs who continue to struggle through the first few weeks of the most minuscule desensitization efforts warrant medication consideration as well, as a way to gain purchase on the problem. Some clients resist the very notion of using medication. To be able to discuss these concerns with your client, you need a basic understanding of the medications used for separation anxiety.

Medications used to treat separation anxiety

Typically, the medications involved are antidepressants. Two medications have been labeled and approved for specific use with separation anxiety: Clomicalm® and Reconcile®. Both medications have been studied for a long time and are also used in human pharmacology.

The things your clients need to know about these two commonly prescribed separation anxiety medications include:

- They are not habit forming.
- They are not sedatives.
- They are not new; they are heavily researched and are safe to use.
- They won't change a dog's personality except to reduce overall anxiety, which may mean the dog becomes even more fabulous than he already is.
- They will likely not have to be permanent as many dogs can be weaned off or put on a reduced dose once the problem has been resolved.
- They aren't prescribed because an owner is lazy and doesn't want to do the work. On the contrary, they support a proper treatment protocol.

Clomicalm

Clomicalm was the first of the two medications to be approved for use in dogs with separation anxiety. It's a tricyclic antidepressant, and it has been shown to decrease anxiety and support a sound behavioral protocol. Tricyclic antidepressants increase levels of norepinephrine and serotonin, two neurotransmitters, and block the action of acetylcholine, another neurotransmitter. For some dogs, Clomicalm is just the bit of help needed to further a behavior plan and resolve the problem successfully.

After the separation anxiety has been relieved, the medication can be weaned off in most cases. The generic version of Clomicalm is called clomipramine. Clomicalm is often the first medication veterinarians choose when asked about separation anxiety, most likely because it has been around the longest.

As with most medications, Clomicalm has side effects. The most common side effects listed by Novartis, the company that produces the medication, are lethargy, vomiting and elevation in liver enzymes. The lethargy, if it occurs, tends to go away after the first week or two in my experience. I haven't personally seen vomiting to be that common, but I know liver enzyme elevation can be of concern and, for that reason, many veterinarians require occasional blood tests to make sure the dog isn't at risk.

Reconcile

Reconcile was approved by the FDA for use with separation anxiety more recently than Clomicalm. It's an SSRI (selective serotonin reuptake inhibitor) whose common name is Prozac® and generic name is fluoxetine. SSRIs like Prozac work by blocking the site where serotonin would normally get whisked away, which allows the serotonin to hang around a little longer. Serotonin is a chemical messenger, and higher levels of it in the brain are associated with mood stabilization which is why SSRIs are such effective antidepressants. In the studies done by the company that produces Reconcile, significant improvement was seen in dogs who took the drug in addition to following a behavior modification program versus those who did only behavior modification (42% showed signs of improvement versus 18%). The research further shows that within eight weeks, 73% of dogs treated with Reconcile showed significant improvement as compared to 51% treated by behavior modification alone (Elanco Market Reseach with Veterinarians and Veterinary Technicians, 2006).

These numbers support the remarkable effects I have seen personally over many years. Reconcile is also a very safe medication with low toxicity, making it an incredible breakthrough in the options available for dogs who suffer greatly.

The side effect most commonly seen with Reconcile is reduced appetite, but this often goes away within the first few weeks of treatment.

Other options

While Clomicalm and Reconcile are the most common antidepressants and the only ones labeled approved for use in dogs, a few others in the antidepressant category have also been effective. Most notably buspirone (Buspar®), paroxetine (Paxil®), sertraline (Zoloft®) and amitryptaline (Elavil®) can also be used.

Mild sedatives

Occasionally, veterinarians recommend that a sedative be used in conjunction with the antidepressant at the outset of the program. Most antidepressants take a few weeks to get into a dog's system (what is known as the "therapeutic level"), and it's during these early weeks that some veterinarians suggest the use of a sedative.

The sedatives are typically from a class of medication called benzodiazepines, or benzos for short. Medications like alprazolam (Xanax®), diazepam (Valium®) and clonazepam (Klonopin®) have different effects in terms of quickness of response and the amount of time they stay in the dog's system, a variable referred to as the drug's "half-life." Sedatives wouldn't typically be for permanent use because of their potential habit-forming properties and, well, sedative effect.

Unfortunately, many dogs experience a paradoxical effect with the use of some sedatives. Instead of relaxing the dog, the drug has the opposite effect and increases anxiety. Consequently, the use of sedatives should be monitored very closely to make sure they aren't doing more harm than good. *Note:* Rarely will sedatives need to be used for owners who are suspending all absences with their dogs during a treatment program.

Acepromazine

This is a medication that is sometimes prescribed by veterinarians as a sedative for separation anxiety. I cannot caution you enough about its use. I call this medication a "chemical straight-jacket" because it incapacitates the body while leaving the mind totally intact and fully able to panic. In some cases it even heightens the senses, causing noise sensitivity, which is very prevalent (actually highly co-morbid) in separation anxiety dogs. This medication, while actually giving the appearance of a calmer dog due to the extreme physical sedation, can potentially sensitize a dog and worsen separation anxiety. It is still prescribed by some old school vets and some newer vets who feel pressured to help the desperate owner, but it is not a help, it is a potential hindrance.

Beta blockers

While not commonly used, beta blockers can be used with separation anxiety dogs with some success. Beta blockers work by blocking the effects of the hormone epinephrine, also known as adrenaline. When you take beta blockers, the heart beats more slowly and with less force. This slower heart rate has shown to help with relaxation and is one of the reasons that stage performers are fond of their use. They are noted to be quite safe if administered in the proper dosage. The most common beta blocker that I have seen prescribed is propranolol (Inderal®).

Clonidine

Some new medications have shown outstanding success. They may not be widely known or used by all veterinarians, but are definitely worth mentioning. Dr. Nicholas Dodman has successfully used one such medication, Clonidine, at Tufts University. Clonidine is a blood pressure medication that lowers the heart rate and thus helps affect relaxation. A few of the dogs I'm currently treating are taking this medication and I'm pleased to see its effectiveness. This is another medication for which I hope to see more research. Its effect in separation anxiety dogs could prove remarkable, particularly when other drugs have been unsuccessful for that particular dog.

Natural/holistic remedies and supplements

Your very best resource for natural/holistic remedies is a holistic veterinarian. He or she will be able to determine the proper combinations and dosages for the dog. One thing to note about natural and/ or holistic treatments: while I have been fortunate enough to see some dogs get relief when treated holistically by a veterinarian, I have also seen clients become discouraged because they used up valuable time and resources with remedies that turned out to be ineffective for their dogs instead of starting with proven pharmaceuticals. As a trainer, it's important to be aware that this is a highly personal choice and one you should respect, whichever way your clients lean.

L-theanine is an amino acid commonly found in tea (mostly green tea). It has been widely studied and is used to reduce mental and physical stress and to improve attention and mood. It is sold for use in dogs and cats under the brand name Anxitane®, which can be purchased online. L-theanine is also available in chewable treats and liquid drops. L-theanine has been used for humans for a long time and can be purchased at vitamin stores.

L-theanine can be ordered from www.swansonvitamin.com for great quality and prices. It can also be found at most vitamin and health food suppliers. Lactium is harder find, so Swanson is a good resource. It is listed as their Women's Anti-Stress Formula.

Alpha-casozepine (Zylkene®/lactium) is derived from a protein in cow's milk. In preliminary studies, it has shown some promise in the reduction of fear and anxiety in dogs. One study states that alpha-casozepine is as beneficial as using a benzodiazepine (such as Valium), but without the side effects of disinhibition often associated with the use of benzos. This is an interesting possibility that I myself have yet to see be effective, but as with a few of the other natural remedies, I find this a safe alternative and worth trying if interested. I have heard from other trainers that its effectiveness is as high as claimed, so I will continue to observe its use with my clients. I look forward to more studies of this supplement, but at this point in time, based on the results I have personally seen, I equate its use to drinking a glass of warm milk before bedtime.

Melatonin is a sleep hormone that affects the sleep-wake cycle. Many dogs do experience some relief of anxiety with the use of melatonin. However, it's quite possible they get this benefit simply because the melatonin makes them a bit more tired. According to Dr. Dodman, melatonin is entirely safe to use. In lab studies it was shown that no amount of melatonin could be given that produced toxicity or overdose.

Rescue Remedy and other such homeopathic products are intended to improve the emotional state of the dog using very small dilutions of plant essences. According to Rescue Remedy's website, the theory behind these plant essences is that ailing symptoms can be cured by a product that would produce the same behavioral or physical symptoms in a healthy individual. They state: Like cures like. No scientific evidence supports claims of value for these types of products, but the extreme dilution of the ingredients renders them harmless. Rescue Remedy in particular is a very popular product in human and animal use, and many claim to have received great benefit from it. I haven't witnessed any such benefit in my clients and would say homeopathic products like this fall into the category of "can't hurt and might help."

Pulsatilla falls into the same category as Rescue Remedy, as it is another homeopathic remedy whose basis is "like cures like." It deserves a special mention here because it has received a fair amount of discussion on some of my online groups as being quite successful in helping relieve separation anxiety symptoms. I am impressed at the number of separation anxiety sufferers who have claimed to have had favorable results using this remedy, and I am always hopeful to get such results with clients who want to pursue homeopathy. Additional herbal medicines that have some favorable results mentioned regularly are skullcap and valerian. As always, your holistic veterinarian is your best resource.

DAP® (Adaptil®) stands for dog-appeasing pheromones. Pheromones are natural chemicals that can act outside of the body of the secreting individual and impact the behavior of the receiving individual. In the DAP product, the chemical is a synthetic version of a hormone produced by nursing canine mothers intended to promote calm, secure behavior. For this reason, the product claims to be useful in dogs afflicted with separation anxiety. A few studies show that DAP has reduced anxiety in puppies in a statistically significant way. One particular study by Gaultier et al. in 2005 compared 30 separation anxiety dogs given DAP to 27 separation anxiety dogs given Clomicalm, and both improved equally. For the most part, my clients haven't reported such benefits to me from the use of DAP, but a small percentage did have impressive results.

Because DAP has been effective in a handful of cases, I do recommend at least trying the spray version (which is the cheapest). I have a bottle of the spray that I bring to my initial consult and I spray the dog's bedding and surrounding areas to see if we might see the dog relax at all. If we do, I then recommend the clients try the diffuser. Another one for the "can't hurt and might help" category.

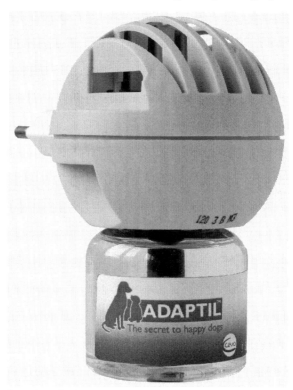

The Adaptil plugin is a great way to go, however the spray is the cheapest version and it also comes in a collar.

Words of caution

Just because something is over-the-counter, holistic or natural doesn't make it effective or safe. Very few controlled studies exist to confirm the efficacy of common herbal remedies in pets, and owners are often swayed by their desire to believe anecdotal "evidence" they may hear from friends or online that has not been subject to scientific research. The same might be said for many drugs used in behavior therapy, but at least most have been proven extensively in studies of humans. Another problem with herbal remedies is that there can be considerable variation in purity and quality from one manufacturer to the next, and even from one batch to the next.

As a trainer, you need to educate yourself about the products your clients are considering using. Many natural products are sold on the Internet where regulations are lax or nonexistent. As an example, I have found several websites advertising stress relief remedies for dogs that contain a tiny amount of minimally active ingredients combined with fillers, alcohol and verifiable junk. At best, these remedies could be a waste of the owner's money; at worst, a dog could have a bad reaction to the fillers and the alcohol. So proceed with care and make certain that scientific evidence and testing have shown the product to be useful and safe for dogs.

Other products to consider

A few other anti-anxiety products and treatments are worth mentioning in terms of use in a separation anxiety treatment plan:

- **ThunderShirt.** The ThunderShirt is a unique tool that can be useful for some separation anxiety dogs. ThunderShirt's patented design applies a gentle, constant pressure that is supposed to have a calming effect for dogs. The important thing to understand about the ThunderShirt is that if it does give a calming effect for the dog, it can't be something that is placed on the dog exclusively for absence times as it will simply become another departure cue. Dogs need to be desensitized to the ThunderShirt to make sure they are comfortable in it and that they are deriving benefit from it. The ThunderShirt is widely available at many pet stores, but also can be found at thundershirt.com.

- **ThunderCap.** The ThunderCap is not likely to be a useful tool for most separation anxiety dogs, but is worth mentioning for those dogs who need some reduction of "visual stimulation" during training. It looks similar to a horse's fly cap; it fits over the dog's head and is made of a mesh that the dog can see through. The ThunderCap should not be used for long durations. You can view or purchase the ThunderCap at thundershirt.com.

- **TTouch Massage.** TTouch, or Tellington Touch, massage and is an excellent way to help dogs get into a state of relaxation. Using TTouch is one way to promote both physical and mental calmness in any dog who experiences anxiety. The techniques used for this type of massage are available to learn through books, DVDs and online videos on sites like YouTube. You can use massage to help an anxious dog get into a relaxed state prior to doing absence rehearsals, but it would be recommended that you do massage at other times as well so that the massage does not become a precursor to absences. To order books or DVDs go to dogwise.com.

- **Anxiety Wrap.** Anxiety wraps work much like the Thunder-Shirt by applying pressure at certain points to promote relaxation. There are many ways of doing an anxiety wrap, and examples of how to create your own abound on the Internet. Everything from complicated bandages going in many different directions down to a simply tied tightly fitting t-shirt can be used. Like with the other products mentioned here, anxiety wraps need to be used at times other than just when absences are occurring to eliminate the potential for it tipping off absences.

- **Through a Dog's Ear.** These are music CDs that are intended to help dogs settle and relax. Developed on the principles of psychoacoustics, these CDs have very specific music on them that is rhythmically arranged to have the most effective calming results. I have been surprised to see the effectiveness of the music in many of my cases. The CD is available for purchase at throughadogsear.com.

5

Management Options

Separation anxiety is generally so debilitating a disorder that management options during the treatment process are absolutely necessary. As mentioned earlier, management strategies alone are often successful in cases that at first glance look like separation anxiety but in fact are just boredom or house-training issues. Only rarely will management alone solve a true separation anxiety case. While some owners might be tempted to employ management strategies exclusively, if you are hired to treat a dog, the options discussed below are to be used to supplement—*not replace*—your behavior modification efforts, and should focus on creative ways to making sure the dog is not left alone during the early portions of the treatment plan.

A little help with absences

The suspension of absences is crucial to a separation anxiety protocol. It is your job as the trainer to help owners find a way to accomplish it. I know through experience that it is possible for motivated owners to do so. Have the owners pull out their schedule, look at every day and find where they need coverage and create a master calendar. Then become their voice if need be. Ask them to pull up a list of email addresses for friends and family, and if necessary you can write an email detailing times and dates of coverage needed. Many people will come out of the woodwork to care for a friend or family member's dog in need if the email is composed correctly. Many owners wouldn't ask these people themselves, but if the email comes from you, that's different.

Next, post a picture of the dog with a heartfelt note about his condition and need for care to the owners' Facebook pages and ask for "likes" and "shares." You just may be surprised what comes of those posts, even if it's not from the direct friend or acquaintance. Be creative, find solutions. College campus postings, ads put up at the local church for inexpensive dog sitting help, community circulars, the list goes on.

Daycare and dog walkers

The training protocol I employ (see Chapters 10-14) requires the owners to be able to spend enough time at home that the dog can remain under threshold during brief (and then longer) absences by the owners. If the owners have to be gone for longer periods of time than the dog can handle, i.e., the dog cannot remain under threshold, then some means of ensuring that the dog is not left alone during the training phase, such as using a daycare or a dog walker, may need to be employed. Such are the demands of work and family. There's nothing wrong with such a choice as long as the dog remains under threshold and the owners have enough time when they are home to work on the recommended training exercises. Some dog walkers are able to take dogs out for multiple walks daily to create enough coverage. If not, using daycare might be a better option. It's important to advise the owner to research the daycare or dog walker in question and make certain her dog is a good candidate for that particular service. Many daycares are excellent, but some are not ideal for a dog with separation anxiety. If the dog can't be crated, for example, and the daycare is crating the dogs for long periods of the day, that environment would be difficult for the dog. One note of warning here: if the dog is excessively shadowing the daycare staff or pacing he may be over threshold and daycare might not be the right environment for him—have the staff observe closely.

All-day dog walkers can be an excellent way to help support a separation anxiety protocol if the right daycare environment cannot be found.

Pet sitters and relying on friends

If the schedule of the owners means they are home most of the time, it's possible only a few absences will have to be covered here and there during treatment. For those owners, using a pet sitter or a neighbor, or ideally a trainer, would suffice. Because you are asking owners to take on the monumental task of never leaving their dog alone during the training period, a really good support network must be put into place to cover all absences. It's important the owners don't feel imprisoned by their dog during the treatment process because this can (and typically does) lead to frustration, which in turn starts to erode the behavior plan. A night off from training once a week can do wonders for both dog and owners. At the very least, encourage owners to find dog-friendly dining options for a night out.

If you as the trainer have to be the voice for your owners by writing emails to their friends, family and neighbors, then do so. Help them look through community postings to find college students or the like who might be willing to cover absences for modest compensation.

See if you can introduce separation anxiety clients to one another so they might exchange dog sitting times. Find solutions in as many creative ways as possible; it's that important.

Take the dog out and about

One way to keep the dog under threshold during training is to encourage the owners to take the dog with them on outings and errands. Many separation anxiety dogs experience little or no anxiety when in the car, so as long as safety and weather permits and local laws are observed, errand running and brief trips can be accomplished while the dog rides along anxiety free. Be forewarned though, leaving the dog alone in the car for longer and longer durations can eventually poison his feeling of safety in the car, so be mindful and use your observation skills.

Leaving the dog alone on the sly

One idea espoused by some trainers is that it's okay for owners to leave their dog for short periods of time as long as they set it up in a way so the dog doesn't know the owner is gone. I strongly disagree with this practice. When it fails (and it most often does), it erodes trust and may make the dog even more alert to absences, triggering even higher levels of shadowing and anxiety. Perhaps a skilled trainer could sneak out on her dog (not likely), but few owners understand what masters dogs are at discerning our presence and absence and won't cover their tracks successfully. Dogs can hear cars from blocks away even when the TV is blaring, so it's folly to think we can tiptoe out.

In the first or second discussion I have with a client, I commonly hear this question in some form: "My dog freaks out when I leave through the front door, but when I leave through the kitchen door, he doesn't seem to notice. Can't I just sneak out that way?" I always tell the client the same thing: Logical as that solution may seem, it would only work for one or two absences. Eventually, inevitably, the dog would sensitize to both exits.

Never lie to your dog. It's that simple. Relationships don't survive lies without damage, and your relationship with your dog is no different. Trust is paramount. I'd rather my clients walk out the front door in broad daylight with their dog watching than have them sneak out and be caught, making their dog ever more hyper-vigilant and ridden with anxiety because he never knows when mom and dad are leaving.

Another dog

Often owners assume their dog just needs some company and decide to get a second dog. Surprisingly, this doesn't help in most cases. Only a small percentage of dogs are relieved of separation anxiety by the presence of another dog, so introducing a second dog into the household is rarely a solution. If you suspect the dog you work with may be helped by the presence of another dog and the owners are interested in pursuing this option, you should audition other dogs and choose these candidates carefully. You don't want your client ending up with two anxious dogs in the home. Or two dogs, one with separation anxiety, one without. The ideal way for an owner to determine if another dog is going to be useful is to not only audition dogs for an appropriate fit but to agree to foster a dog through a local shelter. It's worthwhile to sign up for a few weeks of foster care to learn whether the resident dog is simply performing better because of the novelty of the second dog. If the novelty of having another dog around is what is keeping the anxiety at bay, you will typically see it wear off after the first two weeks have passed.

Even dogs who play beautifully together when you are present may not do so when you are gone. Try fostering to see if another dog helps the separation anxiety before committing to getting a second dog. It is not very common that a second dog helps.

6

Using Technology in Your
Treatment Program

Webcams, PDAs and smartphones have given us a whole new approach to separation anxiety training and monitoring. Technology lets you and your clients monitor the dog so you know how he is doing during absences and can set your criteria accordingly. You can talk to your clients on the phone (or through the computer) and guide them through an absence protocol in real time while watching how the dog is doing on your home computer. Your clients can record these absences so you can point out body language cues (see Chapter 8) and, again, set criteria accordingly with them later (which also makes owners better at looking for body cues and eventually helps them set criteria on their own).

The use of these tools is integral to the treatment of separation anxiety. They remove much of the guesswork about what's going on behind closed doors, and about how much time is too much or even too little. And as you watch from afar, dogs are no longer tipped off by your presence at a training session. Using technology allows you to have greater efficiency, which equals greater success—this is, of course, what we are all striving for.

Technology has allowed me to treat many cases outside my local geographic area. Separation anxiety is one of the few behavior disorders in which the trainer doesn't need to meet the dog or even be present to implement the training. On the contrary, the presence of the trainer greatly affects the dynamic of the absence training, and watching from afar allows for a more realistic setup. I always encourage trainers to see the use of technology as an opportunity to take on clients outside of their regular driving area. I have personally counseled clients around the country and, in a few cases, internationally. The treatment protocol does not change at all when treating from afar versus in person.

I suggest setting up one or two weekly live webcasts with your clients where you walk them through their exercises and point out body language signals and set criteria for them. The rest of the week they can carry out the exercises on their own (with email feedback from you), recording them, if possible, so you can review them when needed.

If you are worried that you or your clients are not technically savvy, don't be. I've never had a single client who couldn't figure out how to use one of these applications, regardless of age. None of the applications that I am referring to here are difficult to use or set up. All that is required is a webcam and a laptop or even a regular desktop. Any webcam will do. Most computers purchased in the last five years have a webcam built in already. If you or the client happen to not have an internal webcam, one can be purchased quite inexpensively. In addition to the webcam, it would be preferable for viewing when your client has a smartphone or a tablet such as an iPad.

As a side note: If the client doesn't have an internal webcam in their current computer, there are many options to choose from including stand alone wireless cameras. Without going into the technical specifications some of my favorites include Dropcam, Foscam and Lorex. These three all have apps that can be integrated to view from a smartphone or iPad by the owner or trainer.

I'll review a few of the easiest applications I use, but many others— for a variety of platforms—are available and can be researched online.

Using webcams and smartphones or tablets to view the dog when alone, you will be able to very accurately set criteria. Additionally, your sessions can be done remotely, which is not only convenient but also quite effective. Here Sylvia is getting ready to do an absence watching her dog Fonzie using iCam.

Skype, FaceTime, Google Hangout, iCam and Presence

If you won't be recording sessions, but only monitoring your clients during live sessions (which is perfectly fine), I suggest you use one of these programs. Skype, FaceTime and Google Hangout are the easiest and user-friendliest of the webcam programs and they can be used with all computer platforms. Again, you won't be able to record your sessions if you use them, it's only for direct, face-to-face communication via an Internet-connected computer. Skype and Hangout can be viewed from most smartphones as well, so the owners can watch their dog during the absence and set their return time according to what they are viewing. Remember to mute the resident computer when using Skype or Hangout so the dog doesn't hear the outside noises through the computer. If both you and your client have an iPhone or iPad, then you can use FaceTime to communicate easily as well, and it is probably one of the simplest of all to set up.

If you and your clients have a tablet or a smartphone, they can use an application I'm particularly fond of called iCam. It's very easy to set up and I highly recommend it, provided recording the sessions isn't a priority. The iCam app allows you and the owners to watch the dog live from your respective locations. The only drawback is that you need to interrupt the live viewing to talk to each other (or send a text), unless you have a second phone. I do use this app often with owners who have iPhones or Androids, because it's so simple to use. At time of writing, it's priced at $4.99 in the app store.

Presence is quite similar to iCam, but the owner would need two Apple iOS devices in order to watch the dog during absences. For instance, she would have to have both an iPhone and an iPad or an iPod, or two iPhones. You as the trainer would need to have an Apple device in order to watch as well. It is a nifty little program if sufficient Apple devices are available, and it is free in your app store.

Ustream

This is a tremendously useful program, it's free and it's my preferred program to use if I require a recording to be made. Owners can record their dog live and you can watch the broadcast in real time or review it later. The live feed can also be viewed on a smartphone. With this setup, owners can watch their dog during an absence and time their return for *before* anxiety sets in. Criteria setting is much more efficient given the greater level of accuracy available.

Note: If the bandwidth isn't high enough, there might be a time lag when watching live feed. A significant delay obviously affects the accuracy of the timing. At the time of this publication, the reliability of Ustream has become quite shaky and they were beginning to add a number of commercials to their broadcasting. If the reliability and speed of this program doesn't return back to its former capacity, this may not be the ideal program.

Vimeo

While I feel the most effective use of video is often live, having recorded video can be useful if live feed isn't available due to poor Internet capacity or if a webcam isn't available for some reason. When this is the case, I use a program called Vimeo where owners can upload regular video from their camera and allow me to view it online. I prefer this way of sharing video over YouTube because it's really private, easy to use and free. YouTube is also free and does have a privacy setting, however it is not nearly as user friendly as Vimeo in my opinion.

For the live training session with her trainer, Sylvia and Kevin use Skype at their respective locations.

The Treat & Train® (formerly known as the MannersMinder®)

The Treat & Train is a wonderful tool that can accelerate separation anxiety treatment. For those who aren't familiar with this training device, it's a remote-activated kibble dispenser. Developed by Dr. Sophia Yin, the Treat & Train wasn't specifically created for separation anxiety treatment, but the device has proved highly successful for this purpose. The Treat & Train remote control can reach at least 100 feet and can go through walls so you are able to dispense even when you are outside while watching the dog from your smartphone or tablet. Additionally, you can put the Treat & Train in automated mode where it will dispense automatically on a variable ratio depending on the time setting you select. It will dispense randomly anywhere from every three seconds up to every five minutes and can continue for hours depending on how much kibble you have loaded it with. For many dogs, it can speed up the training process dramatically. I audition the Treat & Train with dogs at the initial consult to see if this might be a useful tool for them.

Desensitizing the dog to the Treat & Train

Some dogs startle at the noise the turnstile makes, in which case you need to introduce it to them gradually. Follow the steps below when introducing the Treat & Train and watch body language carefully, making sure you create a strong positive association with this clever, interactive device.

Note: The Treat & Train has been designed to use kibble, but not all sizes and shapes work in it. If the Treat & Train is jamming frequently, first change the kibble size or shape. A shape with body mass works best, for example ball-shaped or pyramidal kibble, rather than flat.

> **Step 1.** Set the "tone" switch to "off." (The tone can be left on if desired, but it is not necessary.)

> **Step 2.** Fill the Treat & Train cavity and have it ready to dispense. Check that it works by having it dispense once, but do it well away from the dog so you don't startle him.

> **Step 3.** Place the Treat & Train on the floor and let the dog investigate.

> **Step 4.** Take some kibble or treats from your bait bag, place them in the Treat & Train receptacle so the dog can eat from

it. Allow him to continue to investigate the device. Feed several treats in the bowl without dispensing.

Step 5. Once the dog is no longer concerned about the presence of the Treat & Train, hit the dispense button and then immediately toss a few treats a short distance away from the Treat & Train.

Then:

- If the dog startles at the noise of the turnstile, keep tossing treats a short distance away from the device, and work toward getting him used to the noise.

- If the dog returns to investigate, reward him with treats and dispense again while also rewarding from your bait bag.

- If the dog retreats dramatically, toss the treats farther away when dispensing. Never try to lure the dog closer to the Treat & Train. He will approach when he feels sure it's not something to fear. Continue to build the association between the sound of the turnstile and treats until the dog eats freely from the bowl and associates the noise only with getting kibble.

- If the dog displays extreme fear of the Treat & Train to the point that he isn't desensitizing to it over the course of several 15-minute sessions, you need to consider whether this is the right training tool for this particular dog. In my experience, few dogs are too afraid to overcome the noise of the Treat & Train with time, but it's important to work timid dogs up to a positive association from the beginning.

Lola gives a lovely example of how to lie quietly in front of the Treat & Train, the behavior that I suggest you teach your separation anxiety clients. Lola's Treat & Train is affectionately named Maggie.

When to reward

Only dispense kibble when the dog is quiet, preferably sitting or lying down. I like to ask the dog to go into a down position and then shape him to stay in this position by rewarding only when he chooses to stay down. It happens quickly for most dogs. I prefer them to be in this relaxed position so that when they are left alone in the future, they don't stand expectantly at the Treat & Train for hours. You want to build the association: calm behavior equals food. In the early stages, you will be dispensing often so the dog first understands that a magic food-generating machine has appeared in his world. But you build the deeper association over a few days or, in the case of a really shy dog, a few weeks. The kibble can start to come out more gradually once the dog begins to understand that by settling down and relaxing in a down position, he can control the supply of food. (It's fun to watch the owners' joy when faced with their dog's enthrallment, waiting for that next round of kibble to appear.)

Many dogs will try to get the kibble to come out faster by pawing, licking, barking, nosing and so forth. Particularly the first few times you use the Treat & Train, it is important not to dispense kibble when the dog does any of these things, and to instruct the owners to observe the same rule. The dog has to learn that none of these behaviors work to get the machine to dispense kibble.

Using the remote function

After you finish the initial desensitization, get the remote into the owners' hands right away. During the first stages of the treatment plan, the owners will use the remote to dispense kibble from the Treat & Train so the rewards are well timed for the dog. For instance, the owners should dispense heavily as they walk out of the baby gate or as they open the front door, but not as often when coming back through the baby gate.

Later in the treatment plan, when the association is deeply ingrained and the dog is hooked, you can instruct the owners to put the Treat & Train in variable dispense mode. When using the variable dispense mode, the owners should start at the lower levels (meaning shorter time intervals) and work up to the longer durations, getting the dog even more hooked. Remember that the Treat & Train can be set to dispense at a variable rate as low as three seconds and as high as five minutes and will continue to dispense for several hours. (An example of when to increase the dispense ratio is included in the sample treatment plan #2 in Appendix 3.)

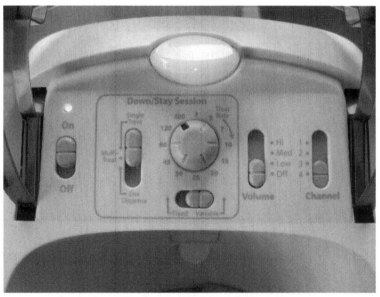

You can see the different variable ratio settings displayed on the dial setting here. It is important to move gradually when increasing the automated variable dispense mode.

A brand new product on the horizon

There is a new product called Pet Tutor that is getting ready to be released that should prove to be revolutionary to use for separation anxiety training. Unlike the Treat & Train, it is a kibble and/or treat dispenser that is smart phone compatible and has programmable dispensing time ratios. Even you, the trainer, will be able to reward the dog from your remote home location with your smartphone via Skype, FaceTime or two way audio webcams. Additionally, the design of this product allows for it to either be on the ground, easily hung inside or outside a crate/gate or placed high up on a shelf so that the dog does not have access to the device itself but will still get fed. Because of the way the product is put together, it is almost soundless, which eliminates the need to desensitize the dog to a noisy turnstile and the product has no problems with jamming. The Pet Tutor can accommodate any size kibble or relatively hard treat and most of the components are dishwasher safe. I am very excited to start using this product. Keep your eye on the release of the Pet Tutor by going to www.smartanimaltraining.com.

There is an app for Pet Tutor for your smartphone in addition to being able to be run it from the remote control or in automated mode.

47

7

Interactive Toys
and Equipment

Owners don't need to buy a great deal of equipment to begin separation anxiety treatment, but a few key items are necessary. The equipment required is of two types: 1) something that will allow you to create a confinement area while maintaining the dog's ability to see his surroundings, and 2) toys that the dog enjoys which can help him remain occupied and calm, creating a positive association with the confinement area while getting used to it during the initial brief absences.

Baby gates / x-pens
Baby gates and x-pens can be a necessary tool in treating separation anxiety in that they permit you to confine the dog both in your presence and out of your presence. If your clients will be buying a new baby gate, tell them to get one that can be left up permanently, meaning one that easily opens and closes like a door rather than one you have to step or climb over every time. Baby gates don't have to be hard-mounted (screwed into the door frame), but can be pressure-mounted, a distinction that can make a big difference for clients who rent rather than own their home.

Another thing to recommend is that your clients get the least noisy gate they can find. X-pens can make a lot of clanging noise and tend to startle some dogs, making the trigger for leaving that much more poignant. Great alternatives to the noisier gates are now on the market—some are downright stylish and fit into many types of home décor. Finally, make sure the door or swinging panel of the gate is easy to open and close (for the owner, not the dog!). A one-handed mechanism is nice; so is a gate that can open in both directions, though that isn't a necessity.

Once the baby gate (or x-pen) arrives, make certain the dog doesn't become afraid of it. Ask the owners to spend a day or two with the baby gate installed but open at all times to get the dog accustomed to its presence without the gate predicting anything. When the dog seems completely comfortable, instruct the owners to close the baby gate while the dog and the owners are on the *outside* of the baby gate with a few treats or a Kong on the inside of the confinement area for a while. You are essentially baiting the dog to want to go into the confinement area which isn't yet a confinement area as far as he is concerned. After the dog is amped up about going in to get his goodie, have the owners let the dog in while leaving the gate open, but not enter with the dog. A simple exercise, yes, but a great way to start building positive associations to the confinement area (more later on confinement area desensitization and counter-conditioning).

You can see from this picture that a nice baby gate which opens and closes like a door is preferred. Also notice that it is set up in a central, comfortable location like the living room or kitchen.

Toys, wonderful toys

Every dog has his preference when it comes to interactive toys. Some prefer toys they can mouth at, others toys they can paw at. Each dog can handle different levels of frustration, and as you are dealing with dogs who have an anxiety disorder, it's important not to push them to experience too much frustration as this can occasionally worsen anxiety. The solution to choosing the right one is to observe what the dog enjoys and prefers versus what he seems indifferent to. This way you can make the most of whichever interactive toys you end up using.

Interactive toys that work well in separation anxiety confinement training are Kongs and/or treat dispensing balls such as the Squirrel Dude, Bobs-A-Lot, Tricky Treat Ball, Kong Wobbler and numerous other variations. You probably have your own favorites; the dogs you work with might, too. Take time to interact with the toys and the dog in question. Many dogs take to the toys immediately, quickly figuring them out on their own and getting rewarded with goodies. But others don't know how to solve problems, most likely because they have never had to. Those dogs give up in mere moments, even on the easiest setting. The resulting helplessness in turn feeds their anxiety disorder. Your job is to teach the dog how to enjoy problem solving and further learning skills. Learning skills are integral to confidence building and empowerment, and most separation anxiety dogs are sorely lacking such skills.

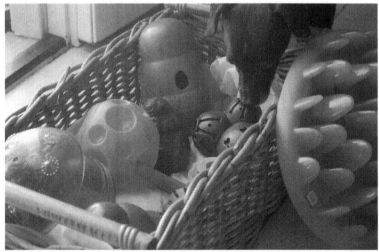

These are just a few examples of the many toys and chews that are available to use with dogs when associating the confinement area with wonderful stuff.

Why food toys?

A question you will hear a lot is, "My dog won't eat when left alone anyway so why are we working on all these interactive feeding toys?" The answer is the interactive feeding toys will be used in such a way to create a positive association with the confinement area. They also serve as great confidence builders for many dogs. While you are still in the house, the dog can learn to love the confinement area, connecting it with all his favorite goodies and playtime with interactive feeding toys. *Understand, though, that you are not teaching dogs to eat when left alone, but rather to relax when left alone.* The interactive feeding toys are simply used as a positive association tool.

While it may seem odd to the owner, once the dog has begun to relax in the confinement area, you need to begin to allow the feeding toy to run out of food to evaluate the dog's reaction. If the dog has access to food while alone, it may mean that the dog hasn't really been desensitized to being alone but merely been entertained for a bit. Running out of food in the interactive feeding toys and learning to relax in the confinement area is thus a key to this beginning stage. I often hear from trainers that they have gradually worked up a dog to 45 minutes of alone time while he's eating a Kong, but when the dog runs out of food he starts barking. A better strategy is to have the food run out after a shorter period of time and then return to the dog a couple minutes later. The time for this work is early on, so the dog can learn to relax without a food toy.

Kong stuffing can become a work of art. There are numerous recipes that can be found on the Internet that include everything from peanut butter, cream cheese, baby food, bananas, canned food, chicken, mashed sweet potatoes, and the list goes on. Get creative!

It does not need to cost much

If your clients are on a budget, any of the items mentioned can be substituted for less expensive or free stuff. Baby gates, for example, can often be found at Goodwill stores or at garage sales or on Craigslist. And while you can buy a plethora of interactive toys that make separation anxiety training easier in pet stores and online, with a bit of imagination owners can create alternatives. Old yogurt containers filled with goodies with the lid tightly affixed and holes punched randomly throughout can substitute some of the expensive treat balls. Cheap tube socks can be knotted up with biscuits inside or morsels of food can be tucked away in cardboard boxes to be shredded during absences and easily disposed of later. Be mindful of dogs known to ingest parts of toys, of course. Safety comes first.

8

The Role of Body Language

One of your primary tools when working with separation anxiety is your ability to accurately read canine body language and to teach your clients to become familiar with it as well. If you aren't fully confident of your skills in this area, I urge you to embark on a study of body cues and work toward mastery. Some good general body language resources include: *Canine Body Language* by Brenda Aloff; *Canine Behavior—A Photo Illustrated Handbook* by Barbara Handleman; *On Talking Terms with Dogs* by Turid Rugaas; and *The Language of Dogs* DVD by Sarah Kalnajs.

You need this skill to do your initial evaluation of the dog and be able to set criteria levels so you know when to move forward and when to stay at the current level—or when to back up a bit. You need to be adept at spotting early signs of anxiety. Once a dog is in full-blown panic—howling, pacing and drooling—you know you have anxiety on your hands and will need to reset your criteria. Fortunately, dogs display many signs long before this stage occurs and a careful observer of body language should be able to avoid panic attacks.

Practice. Get your hands on video of dogs with separation anxiety and watch closely. Looking at dog behavior video not related to separation anxiety can be useful, too, if that's what you can get, as the better ones will help you identify signs of stress. Focus initially on the more common body cues that indicate anxiety. As you become more skilled, you will be able to pinpoint more subtle cues, the so-called precursor cues and stress indicators. In time you will spot cues that are unique and personal to each dog you work with. A few commonly seen body cues that can be indications of stress and anxiety:

- Change in body carriage, including general stiffening or inability to be still.
- Change in ear carriage, dropping to the side or back or pricked depending on ear type.
- Change in tail carriage, progressively tucking or raising stiffly, even quick wagging.
- Change in breathing, beginning to look like panting.
- Change in breathing, including unusual sighs (sounding like precursors to whining).
- Unusual and repetitive yawning and lip licking.
- Displacement behaviors like suddenly scratching.
- Unusual or out-of-place water consumption.
- General restlessness or appearance of searching for something/someone and/or compulsively sniffing the ground.
- Hyper-vigilant scanning of environment.

Here Finnegan began yawning when his owner was doing his first trial separation. When yawning happens out of context, it is a sign of stress.

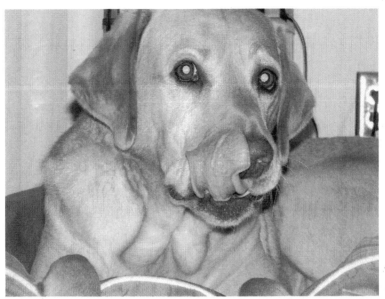

Lip licking can sometimes be subtle little flicks of the tongue or full licks like you see Jared doing here. This is an indicator that the dog is experiencing some anxiety. You should consider this a precursor to anxiety and assume that you are approaching the dog's threshold, particularly if accompanied with other stress signals.

When a dog with separation anxiety breaks into stress barking we know he is over threshold. Sometimes this is accompanied by other "confusing" body language signs like a wagging tail. Don't be confused by that. Anxious barking indicates stress.

It's important to know these cues as well as those unique to the individual dog you are working with so you can begin to adjust your criteria when you notice them. Let's look at a flowchart of what you might experience (see chart on next page). You'll read more about body language in the protocol section later in the book, but this will give you an idea about how the dog's body language dictates your steps.

Say you are working on stepping out the front door and immediately returning. While doing this, you notice the dog is completely relaxed and lying on his bed. Fantastic. You rehearse several times to make certain this particular criterion is sticking nicely before you proceed to the next level. The next step is staying outside the door for one second. Again the dog stays calm on his bed, head down, with a soft, supple body. Based on your observation it seems logical to push it to five seconds. At about three seconds of absence, the dog lifts his head and his ears go up and to the side and he starts to scan the environment anxiously. If you are watching with your phone (see Chapter

6), it would be wise to go back in now, because you can reasonably assume the next thing the dog will do is get up and come to the door. At that point, the anxiety symptoms might start to escalate. From this example, you would likely want to set a new criterion of about two seconds, then work toward a three-second absence based on your observation of the dog lying down without concern up to that point.

If you create an if-this-then-that flow chart as shown below, you would identify all of the dog's anxiety symptoms and their precursors and have flow chart instructions based on each item. For instance, if the dog typically whines and barks, what does the dog do just before this happens? Does the dog display little changes in breathing or miniature whines that might indicate that his anxiety was starting to escalate? Then that would indicate where the threshold is. Dogs who approach the front door or come to the baby gate are another category. Do they approach and sit or lie down calmly (reason to stick with or raise your criteria) or do they get restless, whine and start pawing (reason to lower your criteria). All these subtle cues need to be taken into consideration when you make decisions about moving the criteria to the next level.

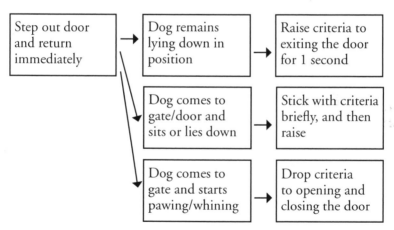

As you can see from this chart, changing your criteria based on the observed body language is important in order to keep the dog from experiencing anxiety. We will address this further in the treatment sections of this book, but make certain you pay attention to the dog's stress signals right away so you can point them out to the owners.

9

The Initial Consultation

Owning a dog with separation anxiety is an emotional rollercoaster. Mixed in with the love and adoration owners feel for their dog, there are moments where they cry over the suffering they witness, moments where they scream in anger at their dog for destroying grandma's beloved antique settee, and moments where they feel they are horrible human beings for considering giving up their beloved pet. It is gut-wrenching stuff and emotionally draining for both dog and owners. Having sat through more sessions with tearful owners than I can count, I can tell you this happens as a rule, not an exception.

At the initial consult, allow enough time listening to your clients' tales of woe. Being a counselor and support person for the owners is an essential part of treating separation anxiety. Owners are usually miserable from the nonstop conflict between their anger about what's happening to their lives and their deep empathy for their dog. Glossing over their feelings and trying to jump right in and start a plan can backfire. Listen to them and make sure they feel heard. (Detailed information on client screening and selection can be found in Chapter 15.)

Questionnaires

Because separation anxiety is such an emotionally charged topic, owners get caught up relating the many stories and examples of their dog's behavior to you, pouring out their frustration and feelings of hopelessness. This will lead to either a very long consult or one where you leave with only half the information you need. Questionnaires are invaluable in keeping you and the client on track during the initial consult. You want to get all the information needed to assess the dog correctly, and having the questionnaire with you allows you to gently push the client along so you can get through the consult and move on to giving management and treatment options.

In my opinion, it's important to fill out the questionnaire at the initial consult, not in advance. Many trainers ask clients to answer lengthy questionnaires in advance of the consult. I don't think this is the right way to go for a couple of reasons. First of all, it can delay your consult, and you need to start working with your clients right away. Second, you need to review the questions with your clients in person as it usually gives you more reliable information. And lastly, many clients resent having spent considerable time filling out a questionnaire you're going to review together anyway.

For a sample initial consult questionnaire, see Appendix #2. Looking at it, you may think you don't need all that information right away—or ever, depending on the severity of the case—but further into your program, the information could well prove crucial. Pick and choose your questions as needed and understand that those that are the most important deal with the dog's symptoms and the client's ability to suspend absences. The goal is to accurately assess the problem so you can get an idea about where to begin your protocol. Does the dog show symptoms the moment the front door is shut or well before? What does the dog's body language look like once the owners leave versus when they are home? You need to know this to accurately assess stress signals. Is the dog stressed at all times, even when the owner is present?

Initial consultation results

The initial consult is a fact-gathering session and by the end of it you should be familiar with the dog's symptoms and understand the severity level of the problem. This is also the time when you ask the owners to commit to at least the next four weeks of working with you and agreeing to suspend absences with the dog. You will also want to get the owners ready to proceed by coordinating schedules and getting a management routine in place by reviewing options like daycare, dog walkers or sitters. If you think a veterinary consultation about medication is necessary, now is also the time to broach this subject. As mentioned in the medication section, if the dog isn't able to settle even when the owner is home, medication can help give some relief. For some dogs in the mild-to-moderate category, you may not know yet whether medication will be necessary. In such a case, it's prudent to wait and assess this after you have worked the program for a few weeks. Typically in this initial consult, if time permits, I like to audition the Treat & Train (and other interactive feeding toys) in the event any or all will be useful tools for the specific protocol you develop for the dog.

By the next time you meet (likely online, but in-person if the clients need help with the mechanics of training), you are ready to start training in earnest.

Spend time at your initial consult reviewing all of the dog's symptoms and the owner's concerns. Remember this is a fact-finding session and the time to set up your goals for the coming weeks, not a major training session.

10

Treatment Protocol: Phase One

Based on my experience, close to 90% of the cases warrant the complete five phase treatment protocol that I recommend, which involves a significant amount of training and behavior modification. Therefore what follows in the next five chapters includes the entire plan.

The steps outlined in Phase One form the foundation of the treatment program. If the owners express concern that Phase One appears to have nothing to do with treating their dog because they don't actually leave during these steps, don't be deterred or persuaded to cut the phase short. Only with a solid understanding and full execution of this phase on the part of the owners can the rest of the program move forward. Skip it and you invariably run into problems later in the treatment.

Goals for Phase One
Setting owner expectations. During this phase you should work to get the owners into the right frame of mind for the program, get them used to the level of work involved, etc.

Building the dog's confidence. Lack of confidence is a major problem for almost all separation anxiety-afflicted dogs and it needs to be addressed for the treatment protocol to be successful.

Tasks for Phase One

- Creating a house layout and deciding on a confinement area.

- Reading assignments.

- Studying body language with the owners.

- Training go to mat and relax/stay behaviors.

- Acquiring interactive toys and equipment.

House layout and confinement area

Take time to discuss what area of the house will work best eventually for the dog during absences. It's not always the place the owners want. Often the owners want the dog to stay somewhere like the laundry room, because there the dog would cause the least damage. However, if it's also the most isolated, cold and uncomfortable place—or it has the most street noise—then it's not the best choice.

Your goal in this first phase is to keep the dog under threshold when confined. If you set things up right, it will be unlikely that the dog will be tearing up the confinement area or eliminating inappropriately. Focus on finding a well-suited area that will be comfortable for the dog. A good choice is wherever the family normally hangs out, perhaps the kitchen or living room. If the dog has an affinity for his crate and you think a crate is the best option, recommend that. I personally use crates sparingly for separation anxiety dogs, although I encourage having an open crate in the confinement space, particularly for dogs already in love with their crates.

Using a confinement area allows the dog to learn to be separated from the owners without them having to leave the house. With a confinement area, you can begin your exercises by teaching the dog to enjoy, or at least tolerate, being separated from his owner prior to being left alone. The baby gate is just a split in criteria, without it you would need to begin the exercises going out the front door with the dog following at your heels. As such, you can allow freedom in the house if absolutely necessary. If the room you choose is difficult to close off with a baby gate because of an open-plan house layout, you can set up an x-pen or have the owners look into buying an extra-wide walk-through gate. Online stores have many options.

Every living environment is unique, and one-bedroom studios present different issues than mega mansions. The thing to remember is that you need an area that can be used as a separate confinement area for practice exercises. Be as creative as you need to—and remind yourself that the process gets easier the more cases you address. Explain to the owner that the confinement area may not turn out to be the permanent place the dog stays during absences, but it's important to have a place where you can teach the dog to be comfortable during rehearsed separations. Later in the program, once the dog is comfortable with separation and with being alone for some small duration of time, the confinement area can be changed or even eliminated altogether.

One last note: I'm often asked whether it's important that the dog see the front door from his confinement area. That choice isn't really up to us in most scenarios, as it's often dictated by the house layout. Either way, it's of no great consequence whether the dog can see the front door; he will still have to be desensitized to the exit routine.

A nice example of Rex getting used to his confinement area by having positive association with all sorts of interactive feeding toys for him to enjoy.

Case study

Chloe's owner, Elisa, wanted Chloe's confinement area to be in a landing area at the top of the stairs right next to one of two exit doors of the condo. Why? Elisa didn't want Chloe to see her leave through the front door, nor did she want Chloe to have access to the front door where Chloe had a history of scratching, howling and barking during absences. But the landing next to the exit door was noisy with building activity that agitated Chloe, and it was tricky to do mock absences from that location since Elisa could not walk anywhere from there except out.

With a bit of persuasion, I convinced Elisa to use an x-pen in the downstairs living room instead. This way, Chloe didn't have access to the front door, but she could see Elisa leaving and returning. We worked through the program without Chloe ever scratching, barking or howling. The fact that Chloe could see when Elisa left and returned was not a problem, because after some time working with her, Chloe remained under threshold and eventually learned to be too busy with her interactive feeding toys to be bothered to watch Elisa leave.

Elisa is happy with where Chloe stays during her absences now. She has bought a gorgeous gate that fits with the stylish, modern décor in her condo.

Reading assignments

It's natural to empathize with your clients. In case after case, you see the anguish they go through and you understand how badly they want to help their dog. I cheerlead my clients tirelessly—I send them supportive emails and remind them frequently what a fantastic job they are doing. However, I'm also relentless about the amount of work I make them do. Not only do I ask my clients to work hard on their exercises and check in with me regularly with notes about what they are doing, the behaviors they notice and so on, but they are required to do some reading as well.

The assigned reading includes handouts and books. I insist on this because *every* dog owner should learn a little about dog behavior and training; for owners of separation anxiety-afflicted dogs, it's a must. I have included the handouts I require my clients to read in Appendix 1. The books and DVDs on body language, such as those mentioned in Chapter 8, and the positive reinforcement training and behavior books I recommend are found in Appendix 4. The goal here is to get your clients to better understand what you are asking them to do in their treatment plan and, most importantly, to have them really understand how to better their relationship with their dog for clear and compassionate communication. Keep your clients learning. It is important, however, that you make certain not to overwhelm your clients. Some clients can handle much more than others, so be observant and adjust your goals accordingly. In the beginning of your treatment plan, the clients will be learning new skills, managing their schedules and reading their plan. If tackling a new book during this early stage might be a bit much, at least feed them a brief handout here and there. As things move forward, ask them to incorporate some additional reading as you see fit. Just like with the dogs, you have to take baby steps with the owners too. More reading and viewing recommendations are included in Appendix 4.

Studying body language

You need to help your clients master the skill of reading canine body language. Part of the desensitization process entails you helping them set criteria, which, as every trainer knows, is crucial if the owners are ever going to work on their own. Show them how they can use their knowledge of body language to determine if the dog is comfortable with some of the key behaviors you will ask the dog to master, such as going to a mat and relaxing (discussed below). Point out body language signals that might crop up during training the dog to stay on a mat (change in ear carriage, displacement behaviors) to the owners so that they can learn to read the signs themselves in the future.

Here are a few of the signals that your clients should master: Can the owners tell the difference between a fully relaxed down and a tight, anxious down where the dog is ready to spring up and follow them in an instant? If the owners walk a few feet away into the kitchen for a glass of water, does the dog follow them, and if so, with what type of tail carriage? How do the dog's eyes look if the owners pick up their keys versus if they pick up the leash? Help your clients to become aware of the different types of body cues and to understand that many of these cues are indicators of stress they need to be familiar with so they can recognize when they are pushing their dog past the point where he is too anxious. In no time at all, they will be masters. The best thing you can do for your clients is to teach them so well that you are out of a job.

Refer back to Chapter 8 for more on the basics of body language that your client should become familiar with.

Training go to mat and a relax/stay behaviors

Phase One contains two behaviors that are critical for any dog suffering from separation anxiety to learn: how to go to a designated place; and how to relax and stay put. Many trainers may already have effective ways of teaching these behaviors, so I deal with them somewhat briefly in the main text but have provided more detailed step by step ways to teach the behaviors in Appendix 3.

Training go to mat 101

Teaching a placement cue as part of a separation anxiety protocol is useful for two reasons. One is that it's essentially a mini-absence rehearsal because you are teaching the dog to walk away from Mom and relax—a great confidence-building exercise that allows you to address a dog's tendency to shadow his owners. The other reason is that the owners need to begin to build some training chops, and this is an excellent exercise for that.

Use whichever method you think will be least overwhelming for the owners. If they have already attended a few training classes and understand clicker training and shaping exercises, then why not make it a fun shaping exercise? If they are novices, on the other hand, don't complicate this exercise and risk frustrating them. Just lure the behavior, get a high rate of reinforcement (for dog and owner), and then switch to a hand signal, then a verbal cue, and so forth.

Always adapt your training technique to your clients' strengths. As soon as you see that the clients understand the concept and process, let them do it. Get the treats out of your hand and into theirs. Better yet, coach them through it from the outset—they learn much more and build confidence if they have to do it themselves. This is key. Confidence on the part of the owner is fundamental to training in general, and crucial to separation anxiety training. If the clients feel overwhelmed the moment you walk out the door, they are doomed.

Remember: You are not there to train the dog, you are there to train the owners. By the end of Phase One, they should be able to succeed in asking the dog to go to his mat from a distance of at least two to three feet.

Here is an example of Ollie being cued to go to his mat.
Notice that at the end he is lying on his mat in a very
relaxed manner rather than in a stiff obedience down.

For a video example of teaching go to mat go to http://www.youtube.
com/watch?v=tjcUNisOqkw&feature=youtu.be

The three D's—Distance, Duration and Distraction

The three D's are key training concepts to keep in mind before you
begin to work with an owner to teach the relax/stay behaviors. One
important thing to remember when working with the three D's is to

never mix criteria, so distance should never be trained while working on duration or distraction. Once all of them are learned well, you can put them together slowly.

Distance. This is the amount of physical distance (inches or feet) you are moving away from the dog when you are teaching a stay behavior. You can manipulate distance very gradually as you work on the stay behavior. Always remember that you should include going to the right and to the left, straight back from the dog and even behind the dog. If you are having difficulty increasing the distance from one foot to two feet, think in inches instead of feet. You can always split things up when necessary. The hardest aspect of the distance component is when moving from in-view to out-of-view. Take it slow there.

Duration. This refers to the amount of time that you are asking the dog to remain in his stay position. You will start with very little duration, just a few seconds, and then gradually build up to several minutes in small increments. Remember to stay right in front of the dog as you begin to build duration initially. You will find over time that you can jump in larger increments, but be mindful that you will likely also hit sticky points wherein you may have to back up and split criteria again.

Distraction. The degree of distraction that you will encounter during your indoor stays is not as concerning as when you practice outdoor stays, however distractions exist in both locations. Distractions can range from simple things such as bending over to tie your shoe or eating a snack, all the way up to the more difficult distractions like the neighbor dogs barking while walking by the window or the UPS man coming to the door. The various distractions that you think might affect your dog's stay should be incorporated gradually into your stay protocol so that he can learn to stay relaxed when they occur. Once he can stay with just distractions alone, you can combine those distractions with distance and duration.

Training relax/stay 101

I call this "relax/stay" instead of just "stay," because I don't want this exercise confused with the traditional obedience-type down-stay. For your purposes, it doesn't matter whether the dog shifts his body weight or changes his position, nor do you need a sphinx-like down. What matters is that it's a relaxed down. The dog's hip rolled to one side is great if that's the position the dog normally chooses, curled up on a mat or bed is even better. It's also not important for the dog to orient to where the owner is. In fact, it's better if he doesn't.

The only goal of this exercise is for the dog to stay in his down. The two important components are: 1) teaching the dog that distance/duration relax/stay exercises are a fun game; and 2) teaching the owner what criteria setting is all about.

Use a special bed or blanket for this exercise. Put it where it will be placed in the future during real absences as you begin building positive associations with the bed now. The "stay" cue will never be used when actually exiting the house; it's simply an exercise to teach the dog to not shadow his owners. And no matter how well the dog knows the cue "stay," start this exercise from the beginning. Ideally you should teach it with a new cue word, such as "relax," which helps remind the owners the goal isn't to achieve an obedience-type stay behavior.

Encourage the owners to get into the habit of noticing and reinforcing the dog when he is lying comfortably on his bed. Whenever the dog chooses to go to his bed of his own accord and relaxes there, the owners should reward him with a treat or with special cuddle time. All the best stuff should happen on that bed. The more positive experiences the dog can associate with his bed, the better. This will give him a place that acts as a security blanket when he is eventually left alone. His bed will become the place he wants to go when Mom and Dad are away, because it's the place he feels most connected to them. Think of Linus in *Peanuts*. That is the kind of connection you want the dog to feel to his bed when his owners aren't around.

Remember: When working on relax/stay exercises, increase the distance and duration criteria separately. And because this is a separation anxiety dog, you need to move along gradually, keeping it light and fun the entire time.

There are detailed outlines of relax/stay exercises in Appendix 3 if you need to refer to them. However, I suggest you adjust the steps to suit the owners, the house and the dog. One thing to note about the steps is that they include varying degrees of difficulty of distance, duration and distractions. You will also notice easy exercises are mixed in with more difficult ones. All dogs are masters of discrimination and pay attention to every detail, but separation anxiety dogs can be even more vigilant than most, so you should never increase criteria in a straight line. During the relax/stay training, show your clients how you are raising criteria slowly and tell them why you are doing so. Point out body language cues and how those cues help you to raise, lower, or maintain the criteria level. In other words, start building their proficiency at criteria setting right away. The better they become at it, the better they will be able to help their dog.

Teaching a relax/stay from a distance can take a little bit of time but holds an important role in the "non-follow" portion of the separation anxiety protocol. Here you can see Ollie understands the "relax" portion of the stay cue.

Phase One recap

Phase One requires a bit of work, probably a few days to a week's worth, depending on the owners' level of understanding and consistency. To expedite things, get them working on several different exercises right from the get-go.

As soon as you have generated a house layout and have determined with the owners where the confinement area will be, start the exercises. Also have the owners jump into their assigned reading immediately. While they wait for the baby gate and other supplies to arrive, they can practice the relax/stay and go to mat exercises.

Tip: At this early point, grab every opportunity to point out body language and to highlight to the owners how you constantly set criteria as you train.

How do you know you are at the end of Phase One? The owners have a beginner-level experience working on exercises with their dog and can get the dog to go to his mat from five paces away. And the dog is learning relax/stay and can endure a ten to twenty second stay with the owner five to ten paces away

Finally, Phase Two can't commence until the baby gate or x-pen has arrived and the interactive toys have been bought or created. All set? Then it's time to forge ahead.

11

Treatment Protocol: Phase Two

Now that you have successfully walked the owners through Phase One, you are ready to integrate in-view barrier absences and to intensify practicing the behaviors you have so carefully installed.

Remember that the dog should be happily and calmly adjusted to the exercises in Phase One before you begin Phase Two.

Goals for Phase Two:
Setting the owners up to understand the desensitization process. During baby-gate exercises and while increasing distance and duration in relax/stay exercises, you will work to develop the owners' criteria-setting skills and help them expand their understanding of desensitization.

Priming the dog to enjoy and relax with an interactive food toy. Many separation anxiety dogs won't eat during absences, but food *can* be a big part of the desensitization and counter-conditioning process to the confinement area. Here the focus is on getting the dog to enjoy interactive food toys so you can benefit from the positive association they will yield.

Introducing barrier training. During this phase, you will slowly introduce the vital step of barrier training. Working the dog gradually up to 30 minutes on the other side of a barrier while in view of the owners is a key goal in Phase Two.

Tasks for Phase Two:

- Working up to a rock-star placement cue and relax/stay.

- The dog learning to love his toys and a fun new game in the form of an impulse control exercise.

- Introducing in-view barrier absences, starting with a few moments and building to 30 minutes.

- Studying body language further.

- Training Treat & Train duration absences (if using the T&T).

- Taking notes (and why your clients should be).

Rock-star placement cue and relax/stay

You have already walked your clients through the beginning phases of go to mat and relax/stay, and they should now have the basic mechanics down. They should also be getting a beginning grasp of criteria setting. This is a good time in the program to let them practice this skill under your direction. Later, when criteria-setting concerns determine the amount of time they are gone during absences, you can't afford to be cavalier about it, so now is the time to let mistakes occur if they are going to happen.

During this phase of the treatment plan, you are having the owners work on both these exercises to the point that they are fluent on at least a hand signal, preferably the verbal cue as well, and you will increase the distance and duration considerably. The learning that takes place during these relatively short absences is paramount. Later, it's precisely the relax/stay and go to mat cues you will use to teach the dog not to follow his owners everywhere.

Most dogs, even non-separation anxiety dogs, follow their owners to a certain degree, but separation anxiety dogs do so obsessively. This is a habit that the training plan will gently discourage by making the not-following practice into a positive. In time, you will have the owners redirect the dog to go to his bed and stay each time he would normally choose to follow them from room to room. As this behavior is practiced and rewarded regularly, and the *game* of it becomes enjoyable, the dog will incorporate it into his own repertoire and choose to not follow his owners. While these confidence-building exercises are very effective for teaching dogs to no longer anxiously follow their owners, you will never be using these cues when you are actually walking out the front door.

In Phase One, the dog had achieved a relax/stay of ten to twenty seconds. In Phase Two, you will have the owners build that duration up to at least one minute. However, be careful. One minute is a long time—easily long enough for owners to lose focus and forget they left the dog in a stay. I recommend asking your clients to get a timer (or use the timer feature on their phone) when they get to this stage.

A tip: Make sure your clients use a stopwatch made for sports versus a kitchen timer. Kitchen timers generally make a loud, obnoxious beep, and most dogs quickly learn the beep means the end of the relax/stay. That's no disaster, but the owners really should initiate the end of the relax/stay, not the beeping noise from the other room.

In this phase, work with the owners to build the distance related to the relax/stay up from five to ten paces away to at least twenty or more. The relax/stay should be enough paces away that the owners can be in view or out of view in another room if the dog can tolerate it. Remember, this is not an obedience exercise. This is about teaching the dog to relax while staying on his mat for one minute while the owners are doing something in the next room, either in or just out of view. The dog has no barriers, no imposed need to stay on his bed, but will learn to stay relaxed and stay in place. That's what makes this exercise so useful: The dog is able to relax on his own, to not follow, essentially learning to self-soothe.

Increasing distance and duration gradually is important. Most dogs can jump from 20 to 25 feet away fairly quickly, but taking an extra step in between not only makes the behavior stronger, it keeps the anxiety at bay and ups the level of relaxation.

Remember: Always increase distance and duration criteria separately. If you increase duration criteria in an exercise, don't increase distance (even better, decrease the distance a bit). And vice versa if you are working on increasing distance. There's a sample outline of how to do this in Appendix 3, but remember to set the steps (or let your clients take a stab at it) according to the level and pace they and their dog can handle.

Learning a new game: Find it
The type of clients you see when working on separation anxiety varies infinitely. Some clients have never taken a puppy class, read a book about dog behavior or even taught their dog so much as a sit. Others

have been through multiple dog training classes over the years and understand many training concepts well.

This means that some of your clients will already have taught their dog some impulse control. If they haven't, it's important they do so now. One of the easiest, most enjoyable and most useful exercises for teaching impulse control with separation anxiety dogs is training the game "Find it." Using the Find it game, you can not only teach impulse control (the dog will be focused on finding treats), but the game is also an ideal way to kick off absences in the future. Different than working hard on a Kong or another interactive toy, the game of Find it allows the dog to quickly enjoy his goodies after a search-and-rescue mission. Teaching the find it game is simple, and the owners and dog usually come to love the game if you show them how to do it in a fun way.

I suggest you have your clients teach the simplest form of this game, i.e., putting the dog in a stay, placing the treat nearby and releasing the dog to find it. Gradually, the owners should build up to longer distances and more complicated hiding places using multiple treats and possibly their interactive feeding toys. If you take this baby-step approach, the attraction of the game for the dog will be powerful. Down the road when the separation anxiety has been addressed, the owners often get great enjoyment from their dog's look of excited anticipation as they get ready to leave—as if the dog can't wait for the owners to vamoose, so he can start looking for his goodies.

In-view (and partially out-of-view) barrier absences

Aren't in-view barrier absences a piece of cake? A waste of time? On the contrary, these exercises are the bedrock of the treatment plan, the little-known link where most separation anxiety programs fail. I can't stress it enough: It may appear the dog experiences little to no anxiety during in-view barrier training and is learning nothing, but you still have to work diligently on these exercises before moving on.

Why? Because if the dog can't be comfortable while the owners are present but out of sight, then working on absences that involve going out the front door is futile. If this step is skipped or rushed through, the common result is a dog who can tolerate a certain amount of short duration absences and then hits an insurmountable wall, for example when he finishes his Kong. Remember, you are teaching the dog how to be okay with solitude, not just to eat a Kong or keep busy with his interactive toys when his owners are absent.

Eventually, the Kong is going to be empty, the Treat & Train will run out of kibble or the bully stick will be consumed. At that point, the dog needs to have the skills to be alone with nothing to do—skills the dog doesn't have and won't develop without help. You need to teach those skills now, at the beginning of the program.

What barrier training looks like
You will find a sample plan in Appendix 3, but the process is as follows:

Initially the owners will learn to desensitize the dog to being placed inside the baby gate within the designated area. Because you are striving to help the dog learn that absences are no big deal—once placed behind or inside the barrier—the initial absences will be barely noticeable and carried out casually. Something to the effect of hanging out with the dog inside the baby-gated area while checking emails or watching the news, and then moving just a few feet away as if to get a glass of water (while staying in view) and returning, all the while ignoring the dog completely.

During this phase, the owners shouldn't interact with the dog at all. That means no eye contact, no consoling, just maybe a few dropped treats as a reward for calm if desired. At the same time, the owners need to closely observe the dog (a tricky balance while maintaining that whole casual attitude) and make notes as to what they observe. Does the dog come to the gate and sit rigidly as they move farther away, and relax as they get closer again? Does the dog notice at all? Does the dog bark within moments of the owners leaving his immediate vicinity?

The next step: food toys
Once the owners are able to leave the dog's proximity for a few seconds and return without the dog showing any signs of concern, you can introduce an interactive toy, chicken strip, bully stick or other goodie. Make sure it's one that will take a little bit of time to consume. Next, have the owners move away from the dog but remain in view in the same casual manner and then return, but increase the time they are gone by five seconds.

During these exits, the owners should be even more conscientious with their note taking. Did the dog stop consuming the yummy treat? If the dog did stop, did he start eating again when the owners got close? You determine the duration of these in-view absences based on the severity of the dog's separation anxiety, but the basic sequence is the same in all cases:

1. The owners hang out for a bit as the dog gets settled (while ignoring the dog).

2. The owners leave the dog's immediate vicinity but stay in view (while ignoring the dog).

3. The owners return and continue to ignore the dog.

The great thing about this type of training is that it fits into most people's schedules. Hardly anyone has to take time out of their day to schedule this exercise, as it can be done while reading the paper or watching a movie. Just make sure you ask the owners to do this training at different times of the day. Many dogs display different levels of anxiety in the evening compared to the morning, and it's important to find out about these differences in case they need to be addressed. I suggest working on the confinement exercises twice a day for about 15 to 30 minutes at a time in the beginning.

Remember, at some point in time during the exercise, the dog will run out of his food item. Make sure you have the owners continue to move away from the dog in the same casual manner and return. You need to teach the dog that the owners' comings and goings are of no consequence, whether with or without the food.

Rex is enjoying his interactive feeding toys in the confinement area, but once he is finished he must learn to rest there happily.

Quick improvements

Even a dog whose anxiety level allows the owners to spend only moments outside the baby gate at the outset can learn to relax for in-view absences of 20 to 30 minutes, provided you build the absences slowly. That means the owners will be able to get that glass of water and also whip up a quick batch of pasta before moving on to Phase Three. Remember, this is all still in view, though a slightly compromised view may be possible at this stage.

The good news is that for many dogs this exercise can be accomplished successfully in a matter of days—or a week at the outside—if the training is carried out carefully. And for trainers who offer day training, this is one component of separation anxiety training that's perfectly suited for you to work on during the day to help accelerate the program.

Two more notes

If the owners use a crate or x-pen instead of a baby-gated area, the process is similar to what is described above. The owners will be hanging out near the crate or x-pen and then leaving briefly while still in view. And of course, before you can use a crate or x-pen, the dog needs to be well desensitized to going in and out of it.

The owners, as always, should be keeping the dog under threshold during this training. However, if the dog whines or barks a little, it's important the owners not suddenly startle and respond by immediately running back to the confinement area. Dogs quickly learn that whining or barking causes the owners to return, and that's the last thing you want. Again, this is an exercise in nonchalance. Nothing the owners do here will put the dog well beyond threshold, so instruct them to pay no mind to the dog if he fusses. Adjust the duration criteria accordingly if the dog is getting too agitated and then build up gradually from the last point where the dog was able to remain calm. Consider rewarding for calm if you are having difficulty making progress. Eventually these mundane comings and goings won't elicit any fuss whatsoever; the dog will be downright bored with them.

Further study of body language

Throughout this phase, help the owners step up their study of body language. If you are working with your clients in person, you can coach them along the way by pointing out key body language points. "Did you see how Lola started scratching her ears after we did several relax/stays in a row? That's an example of the displacement behavior I mentioned." Or: "Have you noticed the way Elle's tail carriage changes just before she starts to investigate the gate and starts her anxiety display? This is her signature precursor to anxious behavior." And a common one that I point out: "Did you notice Redford just yawned and licked his lips for a second before returning to the gate? That's one of his stress signals."

Why body language study is so important

One of the reasons I make such a big deal of teaching owners to read their dog's body language is that the treatment of separation anxiety can take lots of time. Not every owner has the financial resources to pay a trainer week after week, so one of the things I feel compelled to do is put as much of the ability as possible into the owners' hands to know how much progress they are or are not making.

Once the owners can set criteria, read body language and truly understand the process, they scarcely need the trainer other than for emotional support (which is no small part, of course). My primary goal is to get the dog through the separation anxiety, but my secondary (and almost as important) goal is getting the owners to a point where they can continue to treat the disorder mostly on their own, just leaning on me from time to time. (In many cases, there's then a third goal: getting the owners over their personal separation anxiety once the dog is fixed, but that's for another book.)

Once the owners understand how to continue the treatment, they can just check in with the trainer now and again for questions, tweaking the program or moral support. The latter, unsurprisingly, is often the most needed element. Bottom line, the owners can get to know their dog much better than you can through their day-to-day interactions with him. If you can give them the skills to read canine body language, set criteria accordingly and follow a well-organized plan, then you may have trained yourself out of a job, but you know the owners can continue treatment until their dog is better, regardless of financial circumstances.

Treat & Train integration

If you choose to use a Treat & Train in your separation anxiety treatment plan, this is the phase where you will start integrating it. By this point, you or the owners have desensitized the dog to the presence of the Treat & Train and to the noise of the turnstile, and the dog should now be excited about it.

The main differences between using a Treat & Train in a separation anxiety protocol versus just Kongs or other interactive toys are: 1) you need to be mindful of the variable time ratio, and 2) you need to pay close attention to body language to see if the dog is learning to self-soothe. If the dog is so intently focused on the Treat & Train's next payout that he never relaxes, it's impossible for you to predict how he may fare when the Treat & Train is turned off. That's not learning to be alone, that's learning to relax enough to be entertained and distracted. Don't get me wrong; that's not bad, but it has its pitfalls.

What to remember
With you present and in view of the dog, instruct the owners on how to use the remote control for dispensing. The owners should dispense when the dog is showing relaxed body signals as opposed to anxious signals (preferably in a down position).

The initial in-view absences should be brief, and the rate of dispensing fairly high. Reassure the owners that the dog won't always need such a high rate of reinforcement, but in the beginning stages, it's important to set up a strong reinforcement ratio.

Because this is the early stage of the treatment plan, take great care to vary the reward used for in-view absences. Do some using the Treat & Train, some using a Kong and some using no treats at all during the brief, casual exit from and re-entry into the baby-gated area.

This may seem like a lot of exercises, but they are all short and easy to do. Rotating the various exercises in a session, the owners should have no trouble fitting them into the 30 minutes per day they committed to when you began the program.

Note: It is extremely important that you tell the owners not to use the Treat & Train to distract the dog from an activity or behavior they don't want. For example, if the dog gets up and goes to the baby gate and paws at it and the owners choose that moment to dispense from the Treat & Train, they have in effect begun to reward/shape that pawing behavior—exactly the opposite of what you want. It's very tempting for the owners to do this, so explain several times why it's crucial to avoid, and work with them so they can see you reward the dog the first few times. In addition to the Treat & Train, always have a Kong or other interactive toy available for the dog as a backup.

Teaching the dog to stay in a down at the Treat & Train will be very useful for training, but most importantly, make sure the owners never use the Treat & Train as a tool to lure the dog away from the baby gate or front door. They can inadvertently "shape" the dog to go to the front of the baby gate or front door by doing this.

Taking notes

Having your clients take good notes throughout the treatment plan is a good idea for a number of reasons. First of all, you and your clients will be communicating often to set criteria levels for the next steps, and their notes (and yours) will dictate these levels. Additionally, if the dog hits a plateau or sticky spot along the way, good notes can help you identify areas where you can go back and do a little cleanup. And finally, notes can be an incredible comfort. In the midst of a setback or plateau, the owners can refer to their notes and see in black and white the progress their dog has made since they began the program.

Often it's useful for you to set up a numerical scale for your clients, rating anxiety on a scale of one to seven. Using the specific anxiety displays of the individual dog, you can describe each level of anxiety with a number. For instance a one might be no anxiety at all, the dog is lying down peacefully, eyes relaxed. A seven might be panting, whining or barking and pawing at the gate. In the middle of that scale, there would be a level where the dog was still comfortable, yet obviously noticing the absence. This is the point you would instruct your clients never to push past during criteria raises. Owners can then take notes easily after each step by just jotting down a number.

Personally, I always encourage my clients to include an occasional sentence in their notes about how they are feeling about the process. Sometimes it's frustration, sometimes elation. Either way, capturing these feelings serves as an outlet, however small. If that sounds corny to you, consider just how emotional a process this is for the owners. The sheer time and effort they have to put in to see any progress means it's a rare person who doesn't go through emotional ups and downs during a separation anxiety treatment plan. More on this later.

Phase Two recap

In this phase, we have launched into the real meat of the treatment plan. For many dogs, the in-view absences are going to elicit some anxiety. For others, they will be a complete breeze. If your current client's dog is the latter group, breezing right through, don't be fooled into skipping in-view absences—or cutting them short. The exercises still teach the vital skill of self-soothing, even if it's easier for some dogs to learn than others. In such cases, congratulate the owners on their dog's swift progress, and have them carefully observe body language for subtle cues that can help you problem solve during later, tougher absences.

With dogs who are having trouble with the in-view absences, move forward in very small steps. Take the time needed to make the dog completely comfortable with in-view absences before you move on. If you are using the Treat & Train, enjoy the process of teaching the dog to associate the Treat & Train payouts with absences. Often, the dog develops a sense of excitement during this phase that is a pleasure to watch. And remember, the dog is not ready for Phase Three until he is relaxed and comfortable during in-view absences both with and without food. The owners, for their part, are not ready until they easily read their dog's body cues and can tell anxiety signals from relaxation signals.

1 2

Treatment Protocol:
Phase Three

Now that you have completed the in-view steps in Phase Two, you are ready to guide your clients to the next phase. In this section you will begin to set up out-of-view owner absences with the dog. This is a significant step forward and can often be a challenge for some dogs, so again, you will take it slow. In addition, you will introduce the front door into the treatment plan but the owner will stay quite close for this phase, not closing the door behind them quite yet, but just preparing the dog for that actual departure.

Goals for Phase Three:

Begin out-of-view absences exercises. During this phase the owners will incorporate out-of-view absences and basic front-door exercises into treatment plan. At this point, exits from and re-entry into the dog's confinement area have been repeated many times and the dog has become accustomed to the routine of receiving all manner of goodies for being left (almost) alone as well as having time alone after the goodies have run out. What is different now is that: 1) the owner will move out of the dog's field of vision but remain within the house, and then 2) step outside through an open door for a brief period of time. By the end of this phase, the dog should be able to tolerate out-of-view absences for up to 30 minutes.

Making not-following the norm. The not-following routine is now in full use and should be smoothly integrated into daily life in the household.

Incorporating technology. Phase Three is when you introduce technology to get a baseline of the dog's out-of-view behavior.

Tasks for Phase Three:
- Incorporating technology.
- Integrating out-of-view absences.
- Approaching expert body language reading level.
- Taking more notes, including some journaling.

Incorporating video technology

Now, as you begin to work on out-of-view absences, is the time to introduce video technology so that both you and the owners can monitor the dog's behavior when he is left alone. Again, the tools I commonly use include: Skype/Google Hangout; FaceTime; iCam; Presence and Ustream (see Chapter 6).

How to do it
Set up the laptop or webcam in a location so that the camera's field of view can cover as much of the confinement area as possible.

If you are using Ustream, record at least one in-view absence to give yourself a baseline. If you recall, Ustream is an online application that allows you and the owner to view the dog via a webcam on your home computer or on a smart phone. Additionally, the owners can record an absence rehearsal in Ustream if desired. That way, you can compare the dog's body language when the owners are in view versus out-of-view to identify the difference in the signals displayed. The signals may only be subtly different, but they are great to have for future reference.

For some dogs the difference in body language is vast. In those cases, you will have to move the treatment plan forward slowly, starting with extremely brief out-of-view absences or even splitting it further by starting with partially obstructed view absences.

For now, closely study the taped or live broadcast absences and see what the dog is doing during the practice sessions. By the time you get to the next phase—where the owners actually leave the house—you want to be completely familiar with the technology and with reading body language this way.

Out-of-view barrier absences

You will be ready for out-of-view barrier absence exercises if:

- **The dog** is comfortable with in-view absences and is willing to chew on his Kong or get kibble from his Treat & Train when the owners exit the confinement area. He is also comfortable resting there when his goodies run out.

- **The owners** are now showing more ability reading body language and are starting to point out body cues to you regularly.

To begin out-of-view absences with the owners remaining within the house, you can use some everyday household noise initially to allow the dog to orient to the owner's whereabouts. This extra step can help keep the dog under threshold. As for the household noise, you could have the owners wash dishes, walk about while talking in normal voices or something else the dog has often been exposed to. After a few trials, increase the duration of the absences. When the dog seems relaxed about the out-of-view absences, it's time to move on to the front door exercises.

Front door exercises

Most dogs suffering from separation anxiety have learned when the owners approach and open the front door that they are going to be left alone. So the criteria you set in relation to the front door must be broken down into minute steps. For many dogs, seeing the owners simply stepping out the front door, even with the door remaining open, is much too difficult and will cause an immediate spike in anxiety. Determine a number of splits in your criteria that the dog will be able to handle with ease. For example, start by walking halfway to the front door and returning. Repeat this exercise for a while until the dog is quite uninterested in the activity. Your next step might be going all the way to the front door without touching it, and the next might be touching the front door knob, but not opening the door. You might still break it down further by cracking the door a few inches for several repetitions before you get to the point where you are actually opening and closing the door fully. When this has been repeated enough times so that the dog isn't reacting, or is barely paying attention, the owners can begin to briefly step out the front door and then immediately step back in without closing the door behind them.

Note: If the front door is not your clients' main exit door, ask them to use whichever door is. In other words, if they leave the house through the back door most of the time and reserve the front door for special occasions and royalty, then have them practice with the back door.

The number of repetitions you engage in is important. You want the owners to rehearse at each level until the dog is quite relaxed with the activity. Mind you, even dogs who don't suffer from separation anxiety will look up and notice their owners are walking out, so some sort of reaction is normal. You are looking for ho-hum here rather than uh-oh. Go as slowly as you deem necessary. I often tell owners that even if they think they are going slow enough, they should slow down a notch more and that's likely the right pace. In the beginning, owners should set aside two 15 to 30 minute sessions to rehearse their front door exercises. Later in the program, as duration outside the front door gets longer, the sessions will increase in length out of necessity.

In between each of your steps, take time to pause. Pausing between each step makes the activity more realistic and digestible as if each exercise were a cold trial, keeping the dog from ramping up (if that is his tendency) and allowing the dog to remain settled. Don't get too hung up on how long the pauses should be. If you are simply walking to and from the front door, a ten to twenty second pause is perfectly acceptable. Later on, when you have built up to a longer duration and are outside the front door for several minutes or more, you might want to pause for one full minute, but again, don't get too hung up on the length of the pause, just make it long enough so the dog is completely settled and your activity is obvious. Without pauses, your activity looks odd—just walking back and forth to the front door doesn't really look like an absence.

Walking out the front door for the first time is a big deal. The owner must be certain to make the exits very nonchalant as Joe does here with Redford.

Low-key re-entries

Here, as ever, nonchalance is key to success. When the owners return from an out-of-view absence, they shouldn't talk to the dog or even look directly at him. In fact, ask them to imagine being on a phone call or having mail to read for a minute or two before they can greet their dog. The dog should be settled down in his confinement area before he is greeted. Depending on the dog, this may take a few seconds. (If it takes much more than a few seconds to a minute for the dog to settle, then the duration of the out-of-view absence was too long.) And by the way, the owner need not let their dog out of the confinement area after each successive trip to the front door in these early stages. Later on when you have worked up to longer duration absences of 20 or 30 minutes, letting the dog out after he has settled is fine, but in these early stages it is not necessary.

Just as with the exits, the re-entry must also be low key, no effusive greetings and excited hellos here. Just walk in and go about your business, particularly if the dog is excited.

A final word on out-of-view absences

One last note about out-of-view absences: In this phase, the dog must show he can run out of his treats and then settle down while the owners are out of view. And this is true whether you use a Kong, a bully stick or other food toy. Remember, the goal for the eventual real absences is for the dog to not just be consuming food the entire time. Yes, you are creating a positive association with absences by using food, but you also want to make sure the dog learns to settle down without food.

Approaching expert body language reading level

By this point your clients should really be approaching an expert level of body language reading. However, understand that you are now getting into more difficult levels for the dog, so new body cues are going to start to pop up. In other words, you may start to see reactions that you have never seen before, such as the first time the dog paws at the gate or maybe even gives a little whine. Don't be too overly concerned about these behaviors; there's no need to rush to back things up dramatically. Go ahead and continue to rehearse at your current level as long as the new behaviors aren't too severe (if they are, consider a split in criteria). The new behaviors will subside as the dog experiences repetition at the new level and comes to realize that nothing scary is occurring. You are also using technology at this point, so the owners are watching their dog on their smart phone, iPad or computer instead of viewing the dog in person. You are also watching the dog using your computer or smart phone and coaching the client as to what you are seeing in order to effectively set criteria. Watching the dog remotely changes things up a little, so your clients do need to get used to this. The dog may sometimes wander off screen for a moment and the client needs to learn not to panic. The dog may not be clearly in focus all the time, so both you and the owner need to be better at ascertaining the cues of the whole body.

Your goal from this point forward is to be watching the trends in the behavior. For example, with each successive absence is the dog becoming more and more relaxed, nonchalant, or unconcerned? Does the dog become less hyper-vigilant about watching the gate after multiple repetitions? Or do things seem to be ramping up on a particular step with continued repetition? As you watch the behavior trend, it will allow you to dictate how you adjust your criteria, by pushing, dropping or sticking to it. A dog who stays the same or gets a little more nonchalant each time is a candidate for sticking to your criteria and soon pushing it. A dog who ramps up is a candidate for dropping down a criteria level. The degree to which you push, stick to, or drop your criteria is up to you, of course. You will know quickly through observing body language whether your decision was too much for the dog, so err on the side of caution. You can always raise the criteria more later; it's best not to push too much too soon.

Taking more notes, including some journaling

Does journaling sound a little corny? I agree, but I encourage my clients to do it regardless. At the very least I ask them to reflect a bit on how they feel about the process. One client of mine was in the CIA, not exactly the touchy-feely type. I asked him (with trepidation, mind you) to write out at least a few sentences about how he felt after each session. He scoffed. I encouraged. He scoffed more. Because I could tell his frustration, bubbling beneath the surface, was likely interfering with his program, I asked one more time. I told him to send me his notes on his session with one sentence at the end about how it made him feel. Being a good military man, he complied. Within a week I was getting paragraphs of journaling from him and the way he was training his dog changed dramatically. Seems I had given him permission to open the floodgates and acknowledge his feelings of frustration.

Once validated, he was able to replace this frustration with determination, which in turn became confidence and then motivation.

We have to find ways to keep owners from becoming discouraged as their frustration levels grow and turn the frustration around into motivation. A few sentences or so about how they feel can relieve some of this pressure, and kind, genuinely motivating words from you are tremendously important.

Phase Three recap

The work you do in Phase Three desensitizes the dog slowly and safely to out-of-view absences and to activity at the front door. The front door is a potent anxiety trigger for many dogs with separation anxiety disorder, so owners may have to spend a fair amount of time on this phase.

Be ready to encourage your clients. Let them know that what they are seeing is normal for many dogs. And once they have completed this phase they will have a dog who is fine being in his confinement area with the owners out of view for 30 minutes. They will be able to and walk out of the open front door without causing a panic attack in their dog. Plus, if they have stuck consistently to their not-following routine and the dog is relatively savvy, they may have a dog who no longer follows them everywhere around the house, but who often chooses to stay on his own bed.

13

Treatment Protocol: Phase Four

The owners have now built up to a 30-minute out-of-view absence while remaining in the house, which in most cases represents significant progress. They have incorporated many openings and coming and going in and out of the front door along with very brief absences outside with the door open. The dog is able to go his bed on cue and to do a relax/stay for a duration of at least 30 seconds to one minute, two cues the owners have ideally been using every day as a part of their not-following routine. It's time to move on to exiting the front door in earnest and building up some duration outside. In addition you will add in some important cues to the absence so that the dog can desensitize to the real sounds of being left alone.

Goals for Phase Four:
Building up to longer absences. In this phase, you will set succinct criteria as you do exercises in which you build up duration during absences outside of the house (now with the front door closed) to 30 minutes. In addition, you will add in some important cues relating to out-of-the-house absences as well.

Solidifying the dog's independence in the home. Many owners slacken their commitment to the not-following routine during this stage—and you need to make sure that doesn't happen. If the routine has been consistently carried out, the owners should now begin to see their dog regularly choosing not to follow them.

Making the most of technology. You will be relying heavily on web-based technology from this phase forward.

Tasks for Phase Four:
- Increasing time out the front door.
- Introducing out-of-the house absences with door closed.
- Recommitting to the not-following routine.
- Building duration of out-of-the-house absences and adding in cues.
- Using technology to set criteria more effectively.

In most cases, this phase and beyond is where you will spend the bulk of your time. This is probably not surprising to you, as building up duration in actual out-of-the-house absences is key to any separation anxiety program.

Increasing time out of the house

Even though the first several absences out the front door will be brief, some dogs may still display anxiety. Tell the owners not to be too concerned or think all the progress they have made is lost if the dog gets a little upset when they walk out and close the door the first time. This is a big change, and many dogs express their discomfort at first. It may take many repeated absences to desensitize the dog to the owners being outside the front door, so coach them through the process. Encourage them to be patient and help them understand.

Here many trainers err on the side of too much caution where threshold is concerned. True, a dog should never be pushed to the point of having a full-blown panic attack, but if you have followed all the previous steps properly and the dog is a bit uncomfortable here, don't stop, and don't return to a much earlier step. The difference between the owners being on the inside of the front door and the owners being on the outside of the front door is a big mental adjustment for the dog, but persevere.

First, tell the owners to step outside and step immediately back inside several times without entirely closing/latching the door behind them as a warm up, similar to the exercises in Phase Three. Once the dog is completely comfortable with that maneuver, have them step outside, latch the door behind them, and then step back inside. Again, keep having the owners repeat this step; many dogs take several days with this before they are comfortable.

If excessive greeting behavior occurs and the dog can't calm down after a minute, the absence was likely too long and the criteria needs to be modified.

Recommitting to the not-following routine

Just because the owners need to spend a lot of time practicing absences here doesn't mean their relax/stay and go to mat exercises should be forgotten. Hopefully, those are old hat by now. Remind the owners to use relax/stay and go to mat on a routine basis as part of the not-following protocol. The more the dog is encouraged not to follow the owners in their daily activities and the more often he is asked to relax/stay, the more quickly he will progress in his treatment.

If the owners have been carefully following the relax/stay routine, all the repetitions and the reinforcement should be paying off by now. The dog should be loving the game and begin to stay willingly. The following of the owners from room to room should have diminished considerably and the dog should be happy hanging out on his mat.

Introducing out-of-the-house absences with door closed

You have now reached one of the most critical stages of the treatment protocol, the point at which the stage has been set to introduce of out-of-the house absences with the door closed. Being able to leave their dog at home alone successfully for significant amounts of time is why the owners hired you in the first place. There are a number of techniques and strategies that can be employed to help achieve this, including:

- Building duration in small increments, not rushing the process.
- Understanding food consumption patterns while alone.
- Determining the best cues to use when leaving.
- The role of dog walking and day training.
- Anticipating common stumbling blocks.

Building duration in small increments

The only way to get the dog comfortable with the front door being closed with the owners outside is to build duration in small increments. Your chief job as the trainer right now is setting these time increments, because few owners opt to keep the pace of the program slow. Faced with a sliver of progress, most owners push forward to the next level right away. It's your job to help them watch and understand all the body cues so they don't skip ahead too quickly.

Keep in mind during Phase Three the owners were shown here to desensitize the dog to calmly accept 30 minutes of out-of-view absences. The work you need to do now is really no different. Essentially, this is an out-of-view absence, with the owners now on the other side of the front door. You are just asking them to do more of the same thing, albeit in some cases moving along a bit more gradually. If the dog is not progressing, mix in a few out-of-view absences with the front-door exercises from Phase Three and even the in-view confinement area absences from Phase Two as well. If you are using the Treat & Train, have the owners dispense most heavily when the front door is being opened and when on the outside of the front door.

A time will come when jumping large time increments is possible, even advisable, but that's not now. If you think it will help, let the owners know that once the dog can be happily alone between 30 and 40 minutes, you will sanction moving forward in chunks of five to ten minutes. Until then, you hold the reins.

You will find a detailed sample plan for this stage in Appendix 3, but how you end up setting the criteria for the length of time you leave the dog alone greatly depends on the dog. Some dogs need to crawl forward at intervals of a few moments, testing the owners' commitment to the limit and requiring your very best cheerleading efforts. Other dogs are able to move forward in intervals of whole minutes provided you maintain a variable schedule. For example, gone for one minute, gone for three minutes, gone for twenty seconds, gone for five minutes, then opening and closing the door without exiting, etc.

As you no doubt already know, every dog is unique, which is why criteria setting is so crucial. What will determine your success more than anything is your ability to read body language, explain the necessity for trial and error for the owners, be supportive and compassionate and have the best cheerleading routine in town.

Food consumption

Remember that the most important thing you are doing with these dogs is teaching them to be relaxed when left alone, not just to have them eat when left alone. Some dogs won't eat during absences ever, and this is fine. When practicing your absence routine, you want to determine if using the game of Find It with food bits, interactive feeding toys, or Kongs and bully sticks will be useful or not. With many dogs, just having them settled in their confinement area with no additional game or activity is ideal, and you can proceed with the exercises. Choose the activity (or lack thereof) that promotes the most relaxation for the dog. And make certain that when the owners are doing their exercises, they practice for a sufficient amount of time once the food has run out if they are using food. The only exception to that rule is for owners using a Treat & Train. This tool is useful for dogs who react badly when their food runs out. You can wean such dogs off the Treat & Train later when they are more stable about being left alone, but not in the early stages.

Assessing and incorporating departure cues

As the layout of every home is different, you need to determine what types of departure cues (sounds or actions that the dog thinks lead to the owner leaving) should be used to desensitize the dog. For example, if the owners live in an apartment building with a main front door, you have to incorporate that as part of the departure routine once you have built enough duration. If the owners live in a house with a garage—and leaving means pulling out their car—you need to work that in. Simply put, what you will be doing here is adding in these cues at the time that they naturally fall into the routine and making sure to spend extra time there if the dog is particularly sensitive to their use. Some trainers place more emphasis on these departure cues than I do. I find spending tons of time just opening and closing the garage door without an actual departure to be cumbersome and often confusing to the dog. I feel it should be incorporated into the routine at the time in which it would fall naturally, and then repeated to a point that the dog is comfortable.

The same goes for desensitizing the dog to most other departure cues and the entire departure routine. Instead of devoting time to each and every departure cue in the owners' getting-ready-to-leave routine, owners should use their time to build up duration absences. The more obscure absence cues (i.e., putting on makeup or fixing a lunch for the day) can be added in after some duration has been accomplished. Do take note of the significant cues the dog pays particular attention to and incorporate those into your absence. But the absences need to be *realistic*—no need to rehearse wearing bunny slippers—unless you wear them all the time!

The one cue so potent it shouldn't be ignored is carrying keys (and locking the door if that is part of the package). Most dogs use this particular cue to discriminate between real and rehearsed absences, so tell the owners to incorporate carrying their keys from the get-go. Around the time the owners are able to close the door and stand outside for ten seconds, incorporate locking the door as part of the routine. For most dogs, you can add in other departure cues down the line a bit when the dog is comfortable with absences. For example, once the dog is comfortable being left alone for ten minutes, the owners can integrate other departure cues such as bringing a purse or briefcase. When you do this, always shorten the duration of the absences a bit, but generally these cues can be easily integrated with repetition.

Note that the exception to this routine inclusion of pre-departure cues is the dog who is strongly attached to specific pre-departure cues. Typically, these are dogs who have been left alone quite often. I have seen dogs who are fine with brief departures as long as the owner wasn't wearing work shoes, but the moment the work shoes were on, the dog would wildly block the front door or attempt to escape through it. For cases like that, you do need to work intensively on the individual departure cue causing the extreme anxiety. Shoes on, shoes off, repeat, repeat, repeat. There is no need to use treats in this training scenario as this sometimes just gets the dog into "performing" mode as if he is expected to do a behavior. The simple act of straight desensitization works perfectly here. Shoes on, one step toward the door, shoes off. Repeat ad nauseam. Build criteria slowly from this point forward. While doing these exercises, the owner can still work on absences wearing non-work shoes to build up duration simultaneously.

Putting on shoes or jacket, or grabbing your purse or briefcase can be triggers for some dogs, particularly those that have been left regularly and have learned routines. If that happens to be the case for your clients you need to incorporate that into their protocol. For most dogs, however, I genuinely suggest building up duration absences and worrying about the little bits of departure cues down the line a bit. Here, when Erik puts on his shoes and gathers his keys and backpack, his dog Dude gets worried—so repetition of this activity will be required.

Dog walker and day training

At this stage, I highly recommend using a dog walker so you can mix up the timing of absences to happen both before and after the walk. When you have worked up to an out-of-house absence lasting ten minutes or so, you can tell the owners to coordinate their absences with the dog walker. The beauty of this approach is that the dog gets a big reward (the dog walk) at the end of the first absence, and is also introduced to the experience of coming into an empty home at the end of a great bout of exercise to practice the second absence.

Tell the owners to set up their first absence as per the program and to be ready to go about ten minutes before the dog walker arrives. Obviously, the dog walker should be briefed in advance and be on board with the process. She needs to understand that ten minutes *means* ten minutes, not twelve. Time things precisely or have the dog walker silently text the owners when she is ten minutes away. (Silent because dogs are masters of discrimination and quickly learn a phone call predicts the dog walker.) The owners can leave the dog as they usually do and ten minutes later the dog walker will show up for a lovely romp in the park or good long leash walk. The reverse happens at the end of the walk.

The first few times, the drop-off absence may be more difficult for the dog—to be dropped off in an empty home is a new experience—so keep it brief. Tell the owners to have the dog walker leave the dog with something fabulous, like a bully stick, and keep the absence as brief as five minutes if necessary. Within a few practice sessions, the dog will get the hang of the routine and you can begin to increase the duration of both pick-up and drop-off absences considerably. Because the owners are using video throughout this process, you will be able to increase criteria based on what you are seeing. If you see calm behavior over the course of a few days, increase absences on either or both ends of the exercise by several minutes. This process works extremely well to desensitize the dog to 30 to 40 minute absences within a few weeks time, and it also gives the owners a chance to run errands away from the home.

Day training is where a trainer works with the dog during the day while the owner is absent. If you offer this service then consider working in tandem with a dog walker or a daycare. For owners who use daycare because they work during the day, either you or a dog walker can make a huge difference. If the owners can't rehearse more than one absence per day, the trainer can rehearse some for them. Common wisdom says this doesn't work, but that's not the case. I have proven with my clients over and over that rehearsed absences from a third party can help tremendously. The trainer can pick up the dog from daycare or from the dog walker, bring him home, and practice the absences at the current criteria level. And because the trainer is not the key attachment figure, she can often push the criteria a little further than the owners would be able to. Either way, the dog experiences positive absences, and that's what you want to rehearse.

*Dog walkers can truly make a difference in helping to extend
the time of absences on either the front or the back end. I have
been so grateful to many a dog walker for helping out with my
separation anxiety protocols, and the owners typically enjoy the
break they offer for errand running and the like.*

Stumbling blocks

The out-of-house absence phase is where most separation anxiety
treatment programs run into trouble, often even falter and fail. Here's
why: Trainers and owners, on the whole, give up. Not that they can be
blamed for giving up. What do you do if the dog hits a plateau here
and can't seem to be budged?

The answer is perseverance and creativity. Remember, most dogs can
overcome separation anxiety, so when a dog isn't making progress it's
time to switch tactics. Split the timing up in different increments.

Use different food-dispensing toys. Remove food items all together. Change the placement of the barriers or remove them if need be and see what difference that makes. Find whatever thing will let the dog handle brief absences successfully and build on that.

Turn the case on its head by asking yourself a bunch of sleuthing questions. Are the morning absences always more successful than the evening ones? Concentrate on those for a while. Does the dog tend to be more relaxed after having eaten a meal, after recently being exercised, or only when a particular amount of downtime has happened in between each absence? Does adding noise (such as classical music or a white noise machine) to the confinement area help? Is it time to incorporate medication or adjust the dosage?

Good notes from the owners will help you here. Comb through those, searching for things you can change that might make a difference.

Just don't change things all at once. As in any scientific endeavor, you need to change one thing at a time to know what is causing positive or negative results. After you change one thing, for example removing a barrier, wait at least a week before you decide whether it had any affect or not. When starting or changing medications, follow the guidelines for how long they take to reach a therapeutic level.

Using technology to set criteria effectively

At a bare minimum, tape some absences during this phase. That way, you can view them and adjust criteria based on what the dog displayed during the taped session. But if you opt to take your use of technology further and integrate webcams, it can be a huge asset in this phase. You can watch absences live from your location and can tell the owners in real time to stay out longer or return sooner. And well-timed entries can make all the difference if you are hitting plateaus—just one more way to be creative, really. Plus, the owners can watch the dog on a smartphone if they have one and can themselves determine the appropriate duration of absences based on what they see.

I can't stress enough the usefulness of being able to watch in real time versus after the event. Each time you or the owners watch the dog during absence rehearsals, you develop a better understanding of the dog's body language, which is a big advantage. Just don't expect—and wait for—the dog to relax completely. Some dogs never get to the point of snoring on the couch; that shouldn't stop you from moving on to the next time increment. Tell the owners it's okay to move forward as long as their dog is not showing signs of anxiety. A dog who is lying down with head up watching is perfectly acceptable, even those sitting for a while are fine.

Even though I have worked with these cases for over a decade, it never ceases to amaze me how many separation anxiety dogs will sit quietly for hours on end during their behavior protocol before finally relaxing enough to lie down or before putting their head down. It always happens, though, and you can almost always see it coming. It's as if the dog finally realizes that sitting up while waiting for mom is just more effort than it's worth.

14

Treatment Protocol: Phase Five

You know the dog is ready for Phase Five when the owners have built up to 30-minute out-of-house absences that include locking the front door. Based on the variables of the house, they should also have incorporated any relevant cues like garage doors, main apartment building doors, etc. and worked on any serious triggers like shoes, for those dogs who are particularly sensitive to them (see Chapter 13). The frequent use of relax/stay and go to mat should be business as usual in the household. Now you are ready to push the out-of-house absences up to four or five hours.

Goal for Phase Five:
Getting some real headway with longer absences. Work to build up out-of-house absences of four to five hours by moving forward in larger time increments.

Tasks for Phase Five:
- Continuing the non-following routine.

- Using technology to set criteria and monitor the dog.

- Increasing absences in larger increments up to four or five hours.

Non-following and technology

I won't bore you with yet another section on the importance of the non-following routine and of using technology. Suffice it to say that both can mean the difference between a cured dog and one who never progresses beyond the one-hour mark—or even regresses to earlier patterns of anxiety. With that said, let's skip ahead to how—and why—to continue the program to two-hour absences and beyond.

Increasing absences in larger increments

Under your supervision, the owners have built up to 30-minute absences. Now you have a clear path to increasing the duration in larger increments. You no longer need to tell the owners to move forward by mere moments; they can advance to minutes or chunks of five minutes or more. But be sure to still use a variable schedule at this juncture. Keep some absences longer, some briefer, and always avoid a straight succession of increasing duration each time.

If the dog shows anxiety as you increase duration, back up a bit and tell the owners to stay at shorter durations for a brief while until the dog is comfortable there, then try again. And remember that hiccups are inevitable, so be prepared for them. A dog might be fine at 30 minutes, at 40 minutes, at 50 minutes, and then suddenly, at 55 minutes, things go south. Don't panic. Just work at the 50 to 53 minute duration for a while and the dog will eventually desensitize to that amount of time and be ready to move forward. You won't run into setbacks every time, but when you do, know that they are perfectly normal.

As you and the owners march forward with the absences in this phase and find you can make significant jumps forward, please don't make the mistake of calling the dog cured. Yes, the literature says dogs that can get through the 30 minute mark can get through anything. And yes, reaching this landmark is a good indicator of future success, but it doesn't mean the owners can just start leaving the dog altogether. For long-term success, you must desensitize the dog up to a two- to five-hour duration. Again, the owners don't need to do this one minute at a time, but do tell them to schedule time to practice these absences and to stick to the criteria at hand.

When to stop

Why two to five hours? My personal view is that for separation anxiety dogs anything above five hours is gravy at best. It is certainly possible to desensitize a dog to longer absences, but these dogs fare so much better if they get some relief, for example from a dog walker, at the four- or five-hour mark. After considerable time of rehearsing four- or five-hour absences, you could potentially introduce longer absences, but most dogs could use a potty break at that point anyway. However, I know many trainers and owners strongly object to this time limitation, so I do qualify that it's my personal opinion.

Some separation anxiety dogs respond very well to treatment and learn to handle one absence per day—but never progress to two absences. To the owners, that means leaving for lunch and a movie on Saturday afternoon is fine, as long as they don't also make dinner plans. Sorry! Why this happens remains a mystery, but I have seen it often enough to know that it does happen.

Maintenance and owner anxiety

Once the dog can be alone for four or five hours, you need to make certain the owners are on board with the maintenance program. The good news here is that few owners have a problem with this. They have put in so much time and effort already that stuffing Kongs, filling treat balls, playing the Find it game, using the Treat & Train or leaving behind bully sticks are second nature. Interestingly, the bigger hurdle is often dealing with the owners' version of separation anxiety.

Most owners who go through this process with you have spent so much time talking to you, emailing you, adjusting criteria, adjusting their schedule, and generally working their lives around their dog's training program that they develop some anxiety themselves around leaving the dog alone—and leaving you. And let's be fair, they have every reason to be anxious about breaking away from the process that has been such a big part of their lives for many weeks or months. Help them through this time until they regain confidence in being able to leave. It's just as important for them to feel comfortable as it is for their dog. Let them know that if they stick to the maintenance protocol their dog will continue to thrive, and that absences are part of this protocol. Not to mention that it's high time they get to enjoy what they have worked so hard for.

15

The Business of
Separation Anxiety

For trainers, having read the book this far, you may be thinking that you can make treating separation anxiety a major part of your training business. And that is indeed possible. In this section, you will find great resources to help you with the business side of separation anxiety. I encourage you to not skip over it. Take it from me, the business side of this work is just as important to your success as all the other skills learned in this book.

Client selection

Your success, both with the dog and the bottom line of your business, depends on your wise selection of clients. Applying strict criteria to the client selection process isn't distasteful; it's the only way to be effective. Like most trainers, I want to save every last dog, but accepting every case indiscriminately is a waste of your time and your client's money. If a client isn't able to devote the necessary amount of time, money or other resources to a treatment plan, don't take her on. By all means, make your rejection kind and diplomatic, explain your reasoning, give some management options and suggest helpful books and articles (maybe even this book). But to only get a client halfway through a program won't help the dog—and it will hurt your reputation.

Some of the questions you ask as part of your questionnaire during your initial consultations will serve as barometers for an owner's commitment level. A potential client who states that she can't suspend any absences, can't use a dog walker or another outside service, and who has a goal of leaving her dog for ten hours a day immediately isn't a good candidate for a successful program.

Scheduling and pricing

When you take on separation anxiety clients, be prepared to devote a lot of time to your clients—and no kidding. Plan on the initial consultation, where you ask them the questions in the questionnaire and go over what a treatment protocol entails and the client's management options, lasting an hour and a half. You should charge and collect a fee for the initial consultation for your time, and this fee can be a barometer of the client's commitment. After that, you need to create an initial individualized treatment plan, a process also requiring a fair investment of time. I suggest emailing the initial behavior treatment plan within a day or so after your initial consult. (For a sample treatment plan, see Appendix 3.) Then there will typically be a phone consult (or email) to review questions about the behavior plan with your client before you both can get started.

At this point, you will have put in quite a few hours and no major training has yet taken place. See how separation anxiety cases can be time-consuming?

Once you begin the training in earnest, you need to keep in regular communication with your client. Beyond any in-person visits you may need to make, allow for two consults per week (one likely by phone, definitely one web meeting) and a few email check-ins. Each week you will be providing new criteria steps based on the dog's progress. Because of the way separation anxiety training is conducted, it's a good idea to set up pricing by having a fixed fee for your initial consult that covers your in-person consult time, and then switch to a weekly support fee for ongoing training.

Note: I ask my clients to commit to working with me for a minimum of four weeks. I know it will take at least that long to get them to the point where they can effectively set criteria on their own. After that, we evaluate. If the clients feel comfortable moving forward on their own and just checking in with me on an ad hoc basis (paid, of course), great. If not, we proceed with the weekly support fee.

Dog*tec's advise on operating a separation anxiety treatment business

I invited the experts at dog*tec to write this section of the business chapter of this book. Below is excellent advice from dog*tec consultant Gina Phairas on packaging, pricing, scheduling and marketing separation anxiety training services.

The case for separation anxiety services

If you ask trainers about their favorite types of behavior cases, you're not likely to hear too many mention separation anxiety. Which isn't really a surprise. Separation anxiety cases require more client support, often in the form of late night phone calls from frantic owners, and are notoriously long running. Add to that the devastating consequences of failed cases, and who wouldn't rather train a puppy?

Unfortunately (and not surprisingly) separation anxiety specialists are in great need and by not taking these cases, trainers leave a good deal of money on the table. Because so few trainers treat it, SA can be a powerful niche to help grow your business. But SA cases are tremendously demanding, and just as Malena's innovative approaches to treating SA greatly improve case outcome, adopting new approaches to structuring, pricing, and marketing your SA service will be key to business success. With the proper practices in place, you can help dogs suffering from separation anxiety while protecting yourself from burnout.

Structuring SA services

The typical private training model is to charge for in-person time with the client only. This model doesn't work for separation anxiety treatment. These clients need much more access to you, and our current business model leaves SA trainers working untold numbers of unpaid hours providing email and phone support between appointments. This support time, and the time spent reviewing video recordings and adjusting training plans, must be compensated to make taking SA cases workable over the long haul.

Owners struggling with separation anxiety need different kinds of support than the average client. Rather than spending time in their home teaching mechanical skills, most of your time will be spent helping clients understand their dog's body language and reviewing the next steps of the training plan. Clients don't need you there in person to watch them leave the house while they practice an absence. They need you to watch their dog while they leave, to teach them how to gauge when they should return, and to help determine their next criteria steps—all of which can be done remotely. So while you'll need to give these clients more of your time, you'll be spending much less time in your car to do it. Let's take a look at the details.

1. Initial consult

As with most behavior modification cases, you'll need an initial consultation to gather a behavior history and create a treatment plan. Plan for a 90-minute consult, as you'll need to spend some time history-taking, assessing, creating a management plan, and outlining the initial steps of the training plan for clients who decide to hire you on.

2. Training plan development and review

Next, you'll need some time to develop the training plan and to review it with the client. You may choose to review the training plan on the phone rather than doing an in-person visit, but you'll still need to factor this into your fees.

3. Weekly support

Finally, you'll need to provide weekly support to clients. This support includes time for pre-scheduled phone calls, reviewing videotape or watching live absences, emailing criteria steps to clients and emergency phone calls or emails.

This expanded structure allows you to provide the support clients need by building it into your schedule. The next step is to make sure the hours of expertise and support you dedicate to SA clients are properly compensated.

Pricing SA services

In dog training, generally what's good for business is also good for clients and their dogs. That is particularly true when it comes to pricing and packaging SA services. Packaging—requiring clients to commit up front to a minimum number of training weeks—helps you maximize your revenue while ensuring clients purchase enough training and support to put them on a path to success.

A typical weekly support package might look like this:

Three to four days of contact per week / two hours a week of support:

- One phone appointment (30 minutes)
- Review tape or web meeting (30 minutes)
- Email support (two exchanges of fifteen minutes each)
- Emergency support by phone or email (30 minutes)

Time is crucial here. Because separation anxiety is no quick-fix, require that your clients commit to a minimum number of weeks up front (a four-week commitment as Malena does, for example). Because cases don't usually resolve in less than four weeks, committing to less wastes clients' time and money. Making this commitment up front will help clients see the process through when there's a setback or progress isn't as fast as they'd hoped, despite your best attempts to set realistic expectations. Your ultimate goal is to change the dog's behavior and give him and his owner relief from this tragic situation. Set everyone up for success by ensuring there will be enough time to make real progress.

Be clear with clients that four weeks won't likely be enough to wrap the case. But it will be enough to make headway and be able to more accurately predict the total time needed. And as you set up additional weeks after the first four week package, you'll be able to reduce the number of weekly support hours. While many cases will take up to three months to complete, as the weeks go on, you'll be spending less time holding the clients' hands. You'll have taught them how to read their dogs and set criteria steps for themselves; they won't need you as much, which means they'll be spending less. By weeks nine through twelve you'll likely just need time for a weekly check-in and some cheerleading.

So what's the bottom line for the client? Let's look at a couple of examples, keeping in mind that the rates here aren't a specific suggestion of what your rates should be. In this example, I've chosen $100 per hour as a base rate to make the math easy:

Sample package

Fee for initial consult (1.5 hrs) = $150

Weeks 1- 4: 2 hrs per week = $200 x 4 weeks = $800

Weeks 5- 8: 1 hour per week = $100 x 4 weeks = $400

Weeks 9-12: 30 minutes per week = $50 x 4 = $200

Total Cost: $1,550

Cost of replacing carpet and front door = More than $1,550!

This may sound expensive, at least until you compare it to the costs of replacing a front door or shredded carpet. And don't underestimate the impact your service can have on quality of life, not just for the dog, but for the human holding the checkbook, too. Relief from the stress, guilt and frustration of living with separation anxiety is well worth the price of your service.

With a twelve-week commitment, you can also afford to give clients a discount for purchasing the package upfront. We recommend around 10%. The drive time SA cases save you makes this discount easy to offer. In the case of our example, a 10% discount would make the total package price $1,395.

Setting polices for SA services

Payment policies

Packages are designed to help clients commit to the training plan. For that same reason, ask that packages be paid up front as well. By asking clients to make not just a verbal commitment, but a financial one, you increase the likelihood that they'll complete the training. Since SA packages tend to run longer and require larger investments, you'll want to take credit cards. Credit cards will allow clients who don't have the cash on hand to say yes to your service. Taking credit cards is pretty easy these days. You can set up a merchant services account with your bank, utilize online services like PayPal, or go with smartphone apps like Square.

In addition to taking credit cards, setting up payment plans also helps give clients easier access to your services. When setting up a payment plan, be sure the clients understand they're committing to the entire training package, even though they're paying in installments. Your client contract should reflect this commitment and indicate the specific dates payments will be paid, the amount of each payment and the client's signature authorizing each payment. Taking time to review the contract carefully with clients can prevent misunderstandings while pressing upon them the importance of consistency and follow through to training success.

As you approach the end of these packages, you may find some clients reticent to give up their weekly cheerleading sessions with you. They may want to check in when they need a boost or hit a training plateau. These clients feel a bit of separation anxiety themselves. You may be tempted to offer to keep checking in. After all, you've spent a lot of time together and likely feel very invested in their long-term success, but don't fall into the trap of giving your services away. Instead, offer clients who wish to continue with you weekly support time, paid up front, for as long as needed or until they feel ready to stand on their own.

Cancellation policies

Consistency is the key to all training, and that's especially true of SA cases. Not working an SA plan regularly can result in setbacks. Each setback increases the length of the training process and puts the dog at risk for re-homing or euthanasia. The stakes are high. That's why the best cancellation policy for SA cases is a no cancellation policy. Anything less says to the client that it's okay to cancel, in fact that you're expecting them to. And cancelling SA appointments can be tempting, particularly when things are coming along slowly. So be clear with clients that they pay for your time whether they use it or not, and be firm about sticking to the schedule. You need clients to stay focused on the plan and in touch with you so you can help them push toward their goal even when progress feels slow.

Scheduling SA services

Adding all these extra support hours into your schedule may require rethinking how you manage your time in general. A master calendar designed to provide time for all the activities involved in your work can help. A master calendar splits your work week into specific slots for each task, ensuring time for everything without rushing, borrowing from your days off, or watching balls fall from the air.

All trainers need specific time slots for client appointments, blocks of time for business administration (regular emails and calls, billing, paperwork, etc.), time for client preparation like homework and blocks of time for working on marketing.

If you take on separation anxiety cases, you'll also want to add specific time each week for viewing video tape or monitoring online video feeds, either alone or with the client, making support calls and answering support emails, plus the inevitable emergency appointments.

Instead of feeling frustrated by emergency appointments, expect them and build them into your calendar. While it won't always be possible to plan when an emergency might happen, having time for them in your schedule gives you room to move things around when necessary without cutting into personal time or pushing something off into next week or beyond.

Keep proper boundaries in mind when designing your schedule. Even SA trainers should have set business hours and their counterpart: set non-business hours. Let your clients know what these are and turn your phone off when you aren't supposed to be working. You'll help many more dogs over the course of your career if you avoid early burnout from being constantly on call.

Here's an example of what your master calendar might look like if you have four separation anxiety clients per week, assuming two hours per week for each.

	Mon.	Tues.	Wed.	Thur.	Fri.	Sat.	Sun.
8am	*OFF*	*Walk Own Dogs*	*Walk Own Dogs*	*Walk Own Dogs*	*Walk Own Dogs*	*Walk Own Dogs*	*OFF*
9am		Admin	Admin	Admin	Admin	Admin	
10am		**SA Phone / Email Support**	**SA Phone / Email Support**	**SA Phone / Email Support**	**SA Phone / Email Support**	**SA Prep/ Emergency Support**	
11am		Day Train #1	Day Train #1	Day Train #1	Client Prep	11:30 Client Transfer	
Noon							
1pm		Client Prep	Client Prep	Client Prep	Market-ing	Client Appt / Transfer	
2pm		Day Train #2	Day Train #2	Day Train #2	Market-ing	**2:30 SA Client Appt / Initial Consult**	
3pm		*Exercise*			Market-ing		
4pm			**Video Review / Web Mtg.**	**SA Client Appt. or Initial Consult**	**Video Review / Web Mtg.**	**SA Client Prep / Emergency Support**	
5pm		Class Setup	Market-ing	Client Appt. or Initial Consult	*Exercise*	*Exercise*	
6pm		Class	Market-ing	Client Appt. or Initial Consult			
7:30pm		Class	**SA Client Appt**	**SA Client Appt**			

* *Italic* indicates personal activities
* **Bold** indicates SA related activities

113

Of course, this is just an example. This trainer happens to take two day training clients per week and teaches classes on Monday nights, in addition to her four SA clients. Your schedule will need to accommodate your particular mix of services. What's important to note is that each task in this trainer's business has its place—and that she has dedicated time off.

Marketing SA services

So you have some new technology and treatment protocols. You have new ways of packaging and pricing your services. Now it's time for new clients. How will they find you?

Solid community marketing is the most effective and affordable way to market a dog business. Community marketing seeks to show, rather than tell. It provides referral sources and potential clients an experience of your expertise and how you can help, rather than simply announcing your existence the way more passive forms of marketing like ads, business cards and brochures generally do. The first step is to hone your marketing message for the SA niche. Then choose projects that share this message with the right people.

Building your SA message

If you want to increase your SA business, you need a message that takes advantage of this powerful niche. Reaching potential clients by simply saying you take SA cases isn't enough. Your marketing message should offer relief from the problem and the worry it causes. It should focus on outcomes, on change. It should stress why potential clients should call you, not simply *what* services you offer.

Until dogs learn to sign checks, your potential client is the human, not the dog, so your marketing message must let the human know what training will do for them. Tell them the benefits of SA training: Peace of mind that their dog is safe rather than escaping while they're away, relief from the guilt of leaving behind a dog who is panicked, the comfort of knowing they won't come home to destruction they can't afford to fix. Painting a specific picture of how the human's life will be better after training is powerful and motivating. It's also pretty easy with SA. The possibility of being able to leave the house without a doggie meltdown is music to a potential client's ears and is enough to get her off the couch and to the telephone.

So what does it look like to translate the benefits of your service into a complete marketing message?

Niche: Separation Anxiety

Benefits: Relief from guilt, peace of mind, ability to get out more, no more expensive home repairs.

Message: Neighbors complaining about all the barking? Tired of coming home to a chewed up house? Fido's stress when you're gone got you stressed out? We can help. Separation anxiety is a stressful and sometimes tragic condition for dog and owner. Our effective training solutions build Fido's confidence so you can leave him home without worry or guilt.

This message not only stresses the benefits of your services, it tells them that you understand and can help. It paints a picture of training outcomes—being able to leave the dog home without worry or guilt.

Highlighting your SA expertise in your marketing can help you standout from your competition and grow your business. By specializing, you give people a reason to call you over anyone else. And when you help solve a problem like SA, when you make that kind of quality of life impact, clients tend to refer to friends and family for any training needs they have at much higher rates than after other kinds of training. Which means your business grows even faster.

SA marketing projects

Once you've honed your message, it's time to think about how to deliver it. SA cases are most likely to come to you through referral sources, so focus on marketing your separation anxiety niche to vets, shelters and rescues, dog walkers and daycares, and pet stores, ensuring that you'll be the first trainer on their minds when they come across dogs with SA. And don't forget your fellow trainers. Most of them are likely to refer separation anxiety cases on—make sure they know who to send them to.

How to let all of these referral sources in on your specialty? Use community marketing projects that show off your expertise, such as creating a branded handout about separation anxiety. Offer a staff training lecture to vet clinics, shelters and rescue groups about recognizing signs of SA and how to counsel owners of dogs with separation anxiety to get professional assistance from a qualified trainer. Do the same for dog daycares and dog walkers, who are often hired by owners tired of coming home to irate neighbors or chewed door frames. Send copies of your behavior reports for separation anxiety clients to their vets and to the shelter they adopted from (with the client's permission, always). Write an article about separation anxiety for local publishing and/or distribute it among your fellow dog professionals. Create a brochure specifically about home-alone training problems that seeks to educate referral sources and the public about the signs of SA, and what SA is.

The point is to cultivate relationships with referral sources and stay in their line of sight—don't let them forget that you're the SA specialist in the area.

Leveraging your current marketing projects

While working away at your new marketing projects, don't forget to leverage any current marketing efforts to promote your SA services. Chances are you have channels for delivering your new marketing message already in place.

Website

Your website is likely your biggest marketing project and has the largest reach, so don't forget to highlight separation anxiety services here. Use separate pages, text boxes, articles and creative copy to tell potential clients (and search engines) that you're a SA specialist.

When writing about SA on your website and other marketing materials, describe the presenting behaviors, as many owners won't connect the symptoms they see at home with the overall SA assessment, and they may not have encountered the term separation anxiety. Think in terms like home-alone training, house destruction, house soiling or potty training problems, barking, etc.

Newsletters

Newsletters are a great way to tell potential clients, as well as past and current clients, about your SA specialty. Give readers insight into your SA services, write an article about the signs of separation anxiety, or share a client's success story. Let readers see what working with you might be like and how you can help.

Social media

If you already find yourself on Facebook, Twitter, LinkedIn, or other social media channels, leverage that presence to get people talking about your SA work. Use these outlets to let other dog pros know you do this work, answer questions, and post information that shares your SA expertise. Here are some ideas for posts to get people talking:

- Articles on meds or brain chemistry
- New work-to-eat toys
- Games and exercises to build out-of-sight confidence
- Build your own sitter-sharing network
- Create a SA support group

There's a lot of SA work out there, people just need to be able to find you. Strong community marketing can give you the exposure you need to become the "go-to" trainer for SA in your area.

Armed with new tech tools and business strategies, treating separation anxiety can be a powerful niche for growing your training business. And for a dog trainer there is little else as satisfying as a resolved separation anxiety case. After all, we're all in this game to keep dogs happily in their homes.

16

Case Studies

Pumpkin

Pumpkin's Story—A Family Effort

When Eveline and Jen arrived late to the adoption fair with their daughters, they weren't sure if they would find the dog they had seen on Petfinder but, as luck would have it, there she was. Filled with wiggles and wags and desperate to jump up and shower them with kisses, Pumpkin was ready to go to her new home.

From the get-go, Eveline noticed Pumpkin had a difficult time being away from them, and the family began working on crate desensitization training. It took some time, more than a few weeks, but eventually Pumpkin could be in another room in her crate for an hour or so and not whine. The family had read everything they could find on the Internet and strictly followed the rules of ignoring Pumpkin when she whined or barked during their crate-training period and, while it was difficult for dog and humans alike, Pumpkin eventually calmed down. They were lucky—few separation anxiety dogs respond to such a training plan. The problem was, this only got them as far as the other room.

When it came to leaving Pumpkin alone in the house it was a completely different story. Pumpkin started barking and panting and putting up a huge fuss immediately. One time, she managed to pull a nearby curtain into her crate and destroyed it along with her bedding. The family tried ignoring her as they had done during crate training, but Pumpkin was experiencing a completely different level of distress and after just a few days, they knew they had to try something else. That's when they called me.

It was obvious Pumpkin had to start from the beginning. Fortunately, Pumpkin had a genuinely positive association with her crate. Many separation anxiety dogs are crate averse, but Pumpkin seemed to find comfort in her cozy crate so we stuck with that as her safe zone. We started by simply going to the front door, touching it and returning. This was easy for Pumpkin to handle, which is why we started there. (Never start at a level that's anxiety-producing for the dog.) Next we began opening and closing the door. Pumpkin paid close attention to that, so we repeated this exercise for a few days until she became bored with it. By the end of the week, we were able to step out the door, close it and immediately return without Pumpkin becoming concerned—success! In my eyes this was a triumph, but to the owners it felt like it took forever and they asked me repeatedly how this would ever turn into a real absence. Owners commonly feel this way, and it's the trainer's job to normalize the process, empathize, encourage the owners, and even try to make the whole repetitive business a little fun too.

In week two, we added duration. Getting to five and ten seconds was easy, relatively speaking. Going beyond that proved challenging for Pumpkin. After the ten-second mark, we moved along in increments of seconds at a time every few days or so. The owners were frustrated and started to have real doubts this method could work. I encouraged, counseled, explained the science, gave case studies, offered phone numbers of clients who had been through this before, and basically let them vent while keeping them on track. Painfully slowly, we made it to 30 seconds and then hit another plateau.

This was week three, by which time the owners deserved a gold medal for their patience. But that patience was wearing thin as continued progress seemed an eternity away—if even possible. We decided a trip to the vet was in order. Maybe having Pumpkin put on an SSRI would help. We continued with the daily exercises, knowing it would take a while for the medication to take effect and begin to help.

I explained to Eveline and Jen that it wasn't uncommon to have a difficult start. Often we hit plateaus and then get a big jump in duration, and then later hit another plateau down the line. Sure enough, that's what happened with Pumpkin. Suddenly (only a day after the vet visit, far too early for the meds to have kicked in), we saw a noticeable improvement in Pumpkin's demeanor and were able to start raising criteria. In the course of a few days we went from 30 seconds to five minutes, and everyone was thrilled. Over the next week we could increase duration criteria in increments of minutes and by the end of week four, we were hovering around the fifteen-minute mark. Not too shabby!

With renewed optimism and dedication, Eveline and Jen rolled their sleeves up and got to work on their longer exercises. Their goal was to get Pumpkin to the point where she could stay home for a few hours by midsummer. In week five, they started increasing the duration in increments of a few minutes at a time and saw enough improvement to almost reach the 30-minute mark.

Many books and articles claim that if you get to 30-minute absences, your dog can handle being left alone for any amount of time. I personally don't believe that, but I do think 30 minutes is a major milestone, so we were happy and celebrated the big breakthrough.

At this point I told them they could start increasing duration in slightly larger increments of even five to seven minutes. They were thrilled and went off feeling like nothing could stop them. Of course, we hit our next plateau two weeks later at around 55 minutes. Plateaus like this are the hardest. The owners have seen such great success and finally feel like there's light at the end of the tunnel, and suddenly the dog seems to fall apart and their belief is shaken to its core. I jumped back in with encouragement, support, counseling, a review of how the process works, and did what I could to normalize the setback. The plateau was a big one and lasted several days, but we got through it and eventually moved forward again.

In total, Pumpkin's program lasted just about five months. At the end, she could be left alone for four to five hours until the dog walker showed up. Late in her program we had experimented with leaving the crate door ajar, thinking Pumpkin might want a little more freedom, particularly for that length of time. She did great with this and interestingly, while she would come out of her crate on occasion, she most often chose to return to her crate to rest.

Pumpkin is a pretty typical case and I include it here so you can tell your clients with confidence that the first few weeks can be difficult and slow, plateaus are normal and long programs of several months are the rule, *not* the exception. Knowing this up front, they may get through any disappointment and frustration a little more easily.

Pumpkin's family is such a happy one now, and after months of daily interactions with them, I can honestly say that I miss them—and I think they feel the same about me.

Charlie

Charlie's Story: The Challenges of Re-Homing

Gray flecks peppered his muzzle and made him look distinguished and beguiling. The thing was, Charlie was only five—far too young for so much gray. But stress does take its toll, and the gray was the outward mark of the internal anxiety that haunted Charlie's life.

Charlie was fortunate. He landed with a good rescue organization that in turn found him an amazing owner, Ken. The two spent a few days getting to know each other and it seemed a heaven-made match. Buddies from the get-go. Then Ken went to the grocery store. Already walking back up the street to his home, he could hear Charlie's mournful wails. He returned to a scene of pure destruction.

Ken contacted me that afternoon. He was completely enamored with Charlie, but he was also a pragmatic person. He knew he couldn't keep Charlie if it meant never leaving him alone, and he didn't have the time or resources to train Charlie. He asked me what it would take to re-home Charlie. I told him the grim truth. There just isn't a surplus of people who have the time, funds and patience to adopt a dog who can't be left alone. Finding such a home can be next to impossible. Ken was an optimist, though, and he vowed to provide the best possible transition home for Charlie. Until he found the permanent home Charlie needed—and he was uncompromising in his quest for that home to be perfect—Ken would support Charlie financially, send him to daycare and do anything else needed so he would never be left alone.

Ken and Charlie's many other supporters went to work in earnest, posting ads and putting up flyers, getting the word out to friends, family members and so on. A few responses trickled in, but they always ended with, "surely I can leave him for just a short time here and there?" Ken and I had to turn away these well-meaning potential adopters because they didn't fully understand what Charlie's condition entailed. Weeks went by. A handful of amazing people came and went. A lovely woman in a retirement home fell in love with Charlie and almost adopted him, until her children stepped in and nixed the deal, saying it was too much responsibility. The woman was heartbroken, and even Charlie looked sad about that lost opportunity. Weeks turned into months. What little money Ken had was spent and now he was borrowing to make sure Charlie was taken care of. Walkers, daycare providers and trainers all did their best to pitch in. But Ken never lost faith, even when the rest of us began to wonder if Charlie would ever find a permanent home.

It took ten months. A young girl—who worked in a shop that sold sex toys, of all things—was looking for a dog. The other employees all brought their dogs to work. She loved those dogs and wanted her own, and when she saw Charlie's ad, she felt he was the one. Because everyone shared an office and the dogs and people were on site the entire time, Charlie would never be left alone. Ken interviewed the girl and did a site inspection, and he found the environment to be the friendliest and most loving he could have wished for. Charlie's new owner promised Ken he could visit and take Charlie on outings now and again. So finally, Ken handed Charlie over, knowing he had played a crucial role in securing a happy existence for this special dog and, most likely, had saved his life.

The moral of the story? Overcoming separation anxiety is tough, but finding a separation anxiety dog the right home may be even harder. This one had a happy ending, but that's by no means always the case. Ken is the rarest kind of owner (and human being), and Charlie the luckiest of dogs.

Goody

Goody's Story: Medications and Creativity

Goody the Greyhound had the most elegant-looking faux eyeliner I ever saw. Sweet and pretty as she was, her separation anxiety was wreaking havoc in her life. Her tremendous howling had put her owner into an almost comparable state of panic about what to do for her beloved dog. The owner's job entailed working long hours, and although she was willing to do anything for Goody's training, she was limited by the amount of time she could devote to it.

Right away we decided Goody was an ideal candidate for pharmacological treatment. After blood tests and a thorough health exam, Goody's vet started her on a moderate dose of Clomicalm. In the evenings, Goody's owner used what little free time she had to work hard on Goody's exercises. Her hope was that incorporating medication would make a big difference in the overall plan. But time passed without much improvement. Sure, we saw small changes, but they were so small we wondered if they amounted mostly to wishful interpretation. The one area where Goody measurably improved was in her ability to tolerate being in the car while her owner went into a grocery store or coffee shop.

After a bit of time, the decision was made to switch Goody to a different medication, Buspar. Interestingly, we saw changes relatively quickly. Soon Goody tolerated brief afternoon absences between being dropped off by her dog walker and her owner returning home. This was encouraging. Goody still couldn't bear to watch her owner leave, but at least she could handle a brief period at home without company, which told us she would eventually be able to tolerate more absences. We were getting somewhere.

More time passed and again the decision was made to change Goody's medication, this time placing her on Prozac. It took a while before we saw any improvement, but when it came it was significant. Within a month, Goody was able to rest happily in the car while her owner went out for an evening dinner with friends. We were even able to keep Goody happy by loading her up in the car, taking a drive around the block, returning home to the garage and parking securely inside where she slept safely and comfortably while her owner was able to have a social life during her rare free hours. Even better, Goody could now be left alone for the entire afternoon without any problems. "Calm as a cucumber," her owner happily reported each time I inquired. Mornings were still hard for Goody, and desensitizing her to the sight of her owner leaving took time, but after another month on Prozac and further practice of her exercises, Goody was fine and could tolerate even the morning routine.

Not every medication works in the same way for every dog, and you may have to experiment a little. But medications *can* make all the difference. Just ask Goody.

Mookie

Mookie's Story: Noise Phobia and Super-Sleuthing

The combination of dignified Shar-Pei wrinkles and Rottweiler markings made Mookie one of the most charming-looking girls around. Great to snuggle with and a champion kisser. But Mookie had separation anxiety from the first day her owners brought her home from the shelter. The owners worked hard from the outset to help Mookie get a life free of anxiety and she saw minor improvements. But there were severe meltdowns, which seemed to happen at random—and it made no difference that Mookie was the second dog in the home, by the way.

The apparent randomness was what stumped us, because separation anxiety is not an intermittent disorder. A dog doesn't have panic attacks about being left alone some days, but then handle it well on other days. Given that her owner and I had managed to get Mookie to a place where she handled short absences without falling apart, why did she still experience such horrendous fluctuations?

We only had one clue to go on. Like many separation anxiety dogs, Mookie was noise phobic, and we thought a type of noise might be the culprit. The question was which noise? She didn't like the sound of motorcycles or fire engines (who does?), but neither would send her into a full-blown panic.

After weeks of investigation we finally solved the puzzle. The neighbors had a team of gardeners come in once a week. For the most part, their equipment didn't upset Mookie too badly, not even the blowers. But on days where the foreman didn't come along, the gardeners turned cavalier about their job and, instead of watering certain beds by hand themselves, they would set up one of the sprinklers in the back. There, it would bang incessantly on the window just above Mookie's confinement area. It was loud and it lasted for hours, and Mookie was terrified of it. On those days Mookie drooled, paced and destroyed everything in sight. She broke nails and tore her gums bloody.

Once discovered, the sprinkler was never placed in that spot again and the extreme bouts of panic stopped. Mookie's separation anxiety was always there under the surface, partially because of her noise phobia, but eventually her owner was able to leave her alone (or rather with her canine housemate) for a few hours at a time. The lesson here is that understanding the factors contributing to separation anxiety is essential—and that bringing your best Sherlock Holmes routine can sometimes save the day.

Chloe

Chloe's Story: When Lives Are Wrecked

Danika and Jeff, newlyweds, had both recently embarked on demanding careers. Their teeny mutt Chloe was two years old. Chloe had been living with separation anxiety since puppyhood, but her condition didn't begin to rule her owners' lives until six months into the marriage when the couple moved to a new condo. Small and in a desirable location, the condo was part of a new development—and the homeowners' association had strict rules. Jeff and Danika immediately got complaints about the nonstop barking while they were at work. Worse still, they came home every day to blood spatter all over the back of the front door and foyer.

That's when the arguments began. Young, both in starter jobs, and financially strapped, they were poorly equipped to deal with Chloe's distress, which now affected everything. They couldn't go out to a simple dinner with friends because Chloe couldn't be left alone. Danika couldn't go with Jeff to company functions because Chloe couldn't be left alone. Neighbors and the homeowners' association were threatening them, and when Chloe had to be rushed to the vet after breaking a tooth and injuring her mouth during an absence, the vet bill cost money they couldn't really spare.

When the couple met with me, Danika was crying and Jeff was angry. They'd been fighting in the car on the way to our meeting. Jeff was willing to give it two weeks of training, but didn't want to spend more than a few hundred dollars. Danika was willing to give the training process longer, but acknowledged they only had a few hundred dollars to spend. She was certainly willing to spend more; they just didn't have it.

They pleaded with me for advice. I watched the tape they brought me of Chloe being alone and it was indeed heartbreaking. She would spend her entire eight hours either barking while jumping at the doorknob and slamming her petite body into the door in an effort to escape, or collapsing to the ground in exhaustion while panting furiously. She bloodied her nose and sometimes her paws, scratching and scraping at the door. Her owners couldn't take time off from their brand new jobs—nor could they afford a dog walker or daycare and, as Chloe had never been properly socialized to dogs, neither was a good option for her anyway.

My heart went out to Chloe's owners. Their despair, love for the teeny dog, anger, hopelessness and misery were all evident. So I took care to be gentle when I broke it to them what it would take to get Chloe through her separation anxiety. I talked about medications, a private sitter and the training program that would have to be implemented immediately. After going over this and the costs involved, I suggested the possibility of re-homing. They agreed, and at first they wanted to have Chloe placed into a foster home, perhaps through a rescue organization, immediately.

I stopped them, and reviewed the realities. It would be horribly unfair to Chloe to place her into a shelter (if one could even be found that would take a dog with confirmed severe separation anxiety) or even a temporary foster environment, particularly with her lack of socialization to dogs and fear of most people and new environments. And inflicting Chloe's disorder on an unsuspecting owner without full disclosure would be unethical. I had to talk them out of both options and let them know the type of fate that would likely meet Chloe in a shelter environment, where severe separation anxiety is often a death sentence.

This was not an easy conversation by any standards, but not only was it my responsibility to tell Jeff and Danika the truth, however painful, it was my job as a behavior counselor to help them do what was best for all involved. That means validating the heartbreaking decision to let Chloe go, yes, but not in any old way. To place Chloe in a shelter or rescue might have made them feel better, because they would not have had to be the ones to euthanize her, but Chloe deserved more.

Danika and Jeff decided to give themselves one month to search high and low for a home for Chloe, and fortunately their dedication paid off. Danika had a distant relative who had MS and was confined to her bed with 24-hour care. The relative was thrilled at the prospect of Chloe's companionship—and Chloe would never be left alone. After a cross-state road trip, Chloe found herself in a loving new home filled with people around the clock.

Chloe's story ended well, but the reality is that dogs rarely have this kind of luck. In severe cases with limited time and resources, euthanasia is sometimes the most humane option owners and trainers are faced with, as the fate these dogs face in the shelter or rescue environment is just too traumatic.

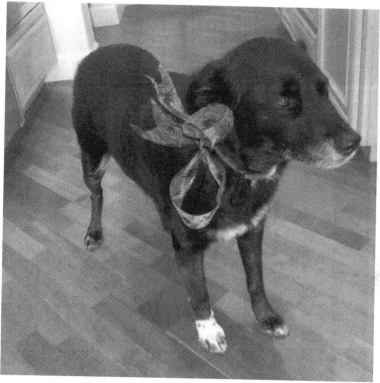

Olive

Olive's Story: Slow Boat to China

Olive, nicknamed Olive Loaf because at the time there was a funny commercial on television about an olive loaf sandwich, is a Border Collie / Lab mix with enough energy for four dogs. And she too was a case of first-day-home-from-the-shelter separation anxiety. Her owners dealt with it mostly by not leaving her alone and after we first worked together, Olive learned to tolerate brief absences. Fortunately, that was as much as she would ever need to be left alone in a busy household with two young children and parents who ran a winery. Olive spent her days at the vineyard with her owners or hanging out with vineyard workers.

Then came the big challenge. Many years later, the winery was doing well overseas and Olive's owners decided to move to China for a few years to market their wines there full time. They contacted me about how to get Olive through this move and how to transport her to China.

Tough one. I'm not a fan of flying dogs in cargo for any reason, but a ten-year-old dog who has been desensitized only to brief absences? Out of the question. We talked about the reality of flying Olive and how it would affect her, on top of the move. That's a thirteen-hour flight, after all.

Realizing that Olive would suffer too much, her owners altered their plans to suit their dog. The mother flew to China with the children; the father and Olive boarded a cargo boat instead for a slow, leisurely voyage across the Pacific. The moral of this story? Never underestimate the lengths to which loving owners are willing to go to spare their dog's needless suffering. I'm asked all the time how I get my clients to commit to such intense training. Well, most of my clients love their dogs the way Olive's parents do.

Final Thoughts

As you know by now—if you didn't already—the process of overcoming separation anxiety involves a great deal of commitment from the owner and from the trainer. Take it from me that at the end of the day, your creativity, persistence and understanding of the client and the dog are what will allow you to get through the protocol and resolve the case. Sometimes you won't see the exact precursor to anxiety, you will have to go with your intuition and push a little. Sometimes you'll get it right, sometimes you'll get it wrong, but as long as you proceed with caution, you can move forward without damage to the overall protocol. When moving through the steps, look for the victories, however tiny, and capitalize on them. Let your clients know what great strides they are making even if they see only seconds of improvement. Seconds make up minutes, which make up hours. Any forward movement is a vast improvement in a separation anxiety dog.

I can't emphasize strongly enough how utterly workable I find this disorder when it's handled properly. I have had my fair share of difficult cases, including some that weren't resolved, but for the most part, even though some cases took considerable time, by far the majority were successes. I urge you to begin taking on these cases. Desperate owners and dogs need you—and helping them is more rewarding than you can imagine.

Appendix 1
Articles and Handouts
for Clients

In my practice I provide all of my clients four handouts. These are:

1. A separation anxiety overview.

2. A listing of eight important things to keep in mind during the treatment process.

3. Learning theory basics.

4. Teaching the go to mat behavior.

Handout #1. Separation Anxiety Overview

From the mildest case to the severest, separation anxiety as a disorder has one underlying commonality: panic. Your dog isn't acting out from spite, he isn't annoyed about your absence, and he isn't trying to punish you for going shopping without him. He is so panicked about being left alone that he can't control himself.

Imagine this scenario. You are driving through a green light, casual as you like, minding your own business. Suddenly a car comes flying through the opposing red light, right at you. You slam on your brakes. The car swerves, misses you by a hair's breadth, then proceeds to speed away. Sitting there, gasping, you notice your heart racing. Your hands shake a little.

Now ask yourself this: In the moment the car hurled toward you, could you have willed yourself to relax? Could you have ordered your heart not to pound? Of course not. You don't have control over the panic that overtakes your body in a situation like that. Nobody does. The brain floods the body with adrenaline to trigger its emergency response. This is what your dog goes through each and every time he is left alone, however illogical, excessive and disconnected from the reality of the situation that response is.

Your dog can't just "get a grip." But he can get better. How? In time, through a type of training called desensitization, your dog will learn that absences need not be a reason to panic.

What you and your dog are experiencing is no anomaly. Separation anxiety affects as many as 17% of the approximately 78 million dogs in the United States.

Like us, dogs form strong social bonds, which is why the typical symptoms displayed with separation anxiety are those a dog would use to avoid being separated from his family: vocalizing, pacing, scratching and Houdini-type escape attempts. As you are probably acutely aware, these symptoms can bring about numerous problems, like complaints from neighbors, costly bills for destroyed property and frightening phone calls about your dog being loose in the neighborhood. Likely you have sought help at this point because you and your dog can't go on the way things are.

Again, your dog can get better. Three out of four dogs with separation anxiety can be completely relieved of the disorder. But the brutal truth is that, compared to the treatment of many other behavior problems, the rate of progress with separation anxiety is slow. You need to know this up front; it will be the most difficult and frustrating part of the treatment for you, because you will see only gradual and minimal progress in the beginning. The learning curve for dogs with separation anxiety can be almost flat during the first few weeks of behavior modification, and only starts to accelerate after diligent adherence to the plan for some time.

Many dog owners give up within the first few weeks. They decide the program isn't working when, in fact, this is when the dog's most important learning happens.

Don't give up. Arm yourself with patience and persist with your dog's treatment.

Handout #2. Eight Things to Keep in Mind

1. It's not personal. Your dog isn't acting out because he is mad at you or to spite you. He has no control over his anxiety or the way he shows it. Even if your dog is perfectly house-trained, his urination or defecation during your absence isn't a way to get back at you for leaving him. He is wetting himself in fear.

2. Logic doesn't apply. While it seems logical to you and me that your dog should understand in time that you always come back (since you always do), he won't. And he won't get over it if you just leave him to his own devices. In fact, a large percentage of dogs get worse as time goes by when the problem is left untreated.

3. Punishment is forbidden. Punishing your dog for chewing the couch, barking, peeing, etc. won't help and will likely make the separation anxiety worse. Refrain at all costs, however angry you are that the antique couch is now a pile of stuffing. Your dog has no idea your anger has anything to do with his behavior and any punishment will only serve to damage your relationship with your dog.

4. Aversive methods backfire. Never use shock or spray collars. For example, if barking is one of your dog's symptoms, using a bark collar to prevent your dog from making noise while left alone is not the solution. Even if his fear of pain from the collar overrides his panic response to your absence, the experience will teach your dog that being alone is even scarier than he thought. Consequently, the fallout damage from using a bark collar can be huge.

5. Flexibility prevails. It's only natural that the peace and quiet of your long-suffering neighbors and the preservation of your furnishings are at the forefront of your mind. But please also keep in mind that your dog is suffering deeply and that ending his suffering must be a priority as well. For this reason, don't get attached to set time lines. Instead, find temporary management alternatives like daycare or an all-day dog walker so you can allow yourself the time to make progress.

6. Patience is all-important. Understandably, you want to know when your dog's treatment will be finished, but nobody can predict that with any certainty. Every dog learns at a different rate, and much of the responsibility rests with you. What can be said with certainty is this: If you put in enough time on your exercises and follow the protocols carefully, your dog's progress will be faster.

7. Drugs or herbs can help. Make sure you know your dog's general state of health and consult with your veterinarian before putting your dog on any kind of medication. Whether you choose to use a supplement or pharmacological intervention, your veterinarian should know that your dog has separation anxiety and that you are embarking on treatment. In some cases, the use of holistic remedies or medication makes sense in the treatment of separation anxiety.

8. Food is a tool. Separation anxiety-induced anorexia in dogs is common. This program makes use of treats and/or your dog's regular food rations, and you might worry about how that will work when your dog won't eat when left alone. No need for concern. Food will be used to help your dog learn to love a confinement area, but the program will not rely on food to be successful later.

Ready to begin your treatment plan? Simply put, the plan will involve training your dog to feel okay about being left alone. We will achieve this gradually through a process that includes confidence-building exercises, departure and absence exercises, exercise and nutrition, and a few other things.

Walking this path will be tough for a time, but can also be fun. And the more fun you are able to have with the exercises, the more quickly the process will go. So have patience and be kind to both yourself and your dog. Not only are you doing the best you can to salvage the couch and prevent the neighbors from egging your door, you are giving your dog the best possible chance to have a life free from the debilitating fear that currently turns every absence into a nightmare for him.

Handout #3. Learning Theory Basics

One of the most difficult aspects of dog training is realizing that progress doesn't happen overnight. Changing your dog's behavior is a slow and gradual process that yields measurable results over time. We humans grant ourselves the luxury of learning things gradually. We read at the *See Spot Run* level for years before we attempt *War and Peace,* for example. Why not extend our dogs the same courtesy?

Being patient with and enjoying the process of training are the two most important qualities you can cultivate if you want good results from this (or any) training program.

Dogs learn through repetition and reward. Behaviors that are rewarded will increase in frequency. The following is a reminder list of the some of the rules of dog training. Each rule applies to the training of any behavior. Understanding these and following them will make your training much more successful. Above all, try to have some fun with your dog as you train!

- **Timing is everything:** Better to let a behavior go unrewarded than to reward it late.

- **Raise criteria gradually:** If your dog is making mistakes often, back up a step until he gets it right.

- **Don't panic at regression:** Sometimes you think your dog has got it down pat, but when it comes to dog training, taking two steps forward and one step back is normal.

- **Vary the motivator:** Don't use the same treats every day. Novelty is priceless.

- **What's working:** Ask yourself what behaviors are working for your dog. What's getting him what he wants? Are those the kinds of behaviors you like? If you don't like the behavior, don't reward it.

- **Patience is a virtue:** True in general and especially true in dog training. Enjoy the process and focus on the small steps of progress rather than the distance to your final goal, great as it sometimes can seem. Allow your dog to learn at his own pace, and give yourself that license, too. Training should be fun and simple, and when it's not, stop. You can return to it again another time when you feel more relaxed and ready to give it another go.

Handout #4 Teaching go to mat

Why teach go to mat? First and foremost, the exercise is a useful tool for separation anxiety treatment, because your dog learns that moving away from you can be a positive experience. Eventually, when your dog is really good at the exercise, you can ask him to go to his mat for a variety of reasons. As you have created such a positive association with his bed, your dog will feel confident about complying with your request and comfortable once he is there.

Getting your dog to go to his mat is simple, but as with all behaviors you must teach it gradually. You start out standing next to your dog's bed and using a lure, but slowly, over several repetitions, you stop using the lure and move farther away.

Before you begin: Chop up some yummy treats to the size of a pea for medium-to-large dogs, and half that for small dogs. Get your dog's comfy bed or blanket ready—and be sure to use the same bed in the same location each time. (Eventually you can use other beds and/or move the bed around, but right now we keep it simple.)

Step 1: Luring your dog onto the mat

1. Stand just in front of the mat, and hold a treat in your hand without showing it upfront.

2. Hold your hand with the treat in front of your dog's nose and lure him to the bed and into a down position.

3. Once your dog is on his bed and lying down, praise him (or click the clicker, if you use one), and give him the treat.

4. Repeat the exercise at least five times. After five successful trials, move on to Step 2.

Step 2: Fading the lure, but use hand signals

1. With your empty hand at his nose in the same position and manner as if you had a treat in it, prompt the dog to the mat and into a down. (Remember: Don't physically push your dog down, just use your hand to show him what you want him to do.)

2. When your dog lies down, give him a treat.

3. Repeat the exercise about ten times. Once you see your dog anticipating your hand request and rushing to his bed, move on to Step 3. (He should get at least eight out of the ten repetitions before moving on to the next step. If not, keep practicing.)

Step 3: Adding in the verbal cue

1. Tell your dog "Mat!" Pause for a moment. (Choose whatever cue word or phrase you want, just stay consistent with it.)

2. Point your dog to the bed with your empty treat hand.

3. When your dog lies down, give him the treat.

4. Repeat the exercise about ten times. Once you see your dog anticipating your request and rushing to his bed, you can move on. (He should get at least eight out of the ten repetitions before moving on to the next step. If not, keep practicing.)

Now you are ready to use your hand signal as a regular pointing gesture. You can fade your hand signal altogether and use just the verbal if you prefer, but it isn't necessary; sticking with a hand signal is perfectly fine.

When your dog jumps eagerly onto his bed and lies down, either from a subtle hand signal or the verbal cue alone, you can begin to move farther away from the bed and ask your dog to go to his mat from different distances and places. Be patient, though. It takes time to work up to that point, so do things in baby steps and always be prepared to go back to a slightly easier level as necessary.

Remember, this exercise should be fun for both you and your dog. Treat this as though you are teaching your dog how to high five or roll over. And if he really doesn't seem to get it, don't assume he can't learn. You just need to break the steps down even further—or you need better treats! Don't be afraid to break out the meatballs or the smelly cheese.

Keep it fun, light, and creative, and soon you will see results that will benefit your treatment plan tremendously.

Appendix 2
Initial Questionnaire

Date:

Client name/s:

Client address:

Dog's name:

Breed type(s):

Dog's age:

Age of dog when acquired and place dog was acquired from (shelter, breeder, etc.):

How many human members in your household? (Note # of males, females and age of children)

How many animal members in your household? (Note # of dogs, cats, and their ages)

If you have more than one dog in your household, are your dogs able to share food and toys without confrontation?

Has your dog always shown symptoms of separation anxiety?

If yes, describe whether the anxiety has improved, stayed the same, or worsened over time:

If no, indicate whatever precipitating events may have caused the separation anxiety:

Check any of the following symptoms your dog displays when left alone at home:

□ Whining

□ Barking

□ Howling

□ Urination/defecation

□ Chewing/destruction

□ Self-mutilation

□ Pawing/destruction

□ Drooling

□ Panting

□ Sweaty paws

□ Pacing

□ Excessive water consumption (upon return home)

□ Trembling prior to departure

□ Excessive greeting behaviors (upon return home)

□ Anorexia

□ Aggression

Describe any other symptoms you have witnessed:

Does your dog display signs of separation anxiety if you are in another room with the door closed?

Does your dog follow you from room to room?

How often do you leave your dog alone?

If your dog is being left alone, how long are the absences?

If your dog is being left alone, where does he/she stay? (i.e., a crate/ the whole house/a bedroom)

If your dog is being left alone, will your dog eat treats/food/chewies/ Kongs during absences?

Does your dog display signs of separation anxiety if others are present (i.e., a friend at your house)?

Does your dog display signs of separation anxiety if left alone in the car?

If your dog does experience separation anxiety while in the car, are the symptoms as severe as when left at home?

Have you ever done any crate training with your dog?

If yes, is your dog comfortable in a crate when you are home (describe if needed):

Can you close the bathroom door while taking a shower? If yes, where is your dog when you come out of the bathroom?

What type of exercise does your dog get, and how often?

Does your dog have any medical issues you are aware of?

List all medications your dog is currently taking.

If your dog has had any serious medical conditions in the past year, describe them and list any medications used.

Have you done any type of formal training with your dog? (Classes/ private trainer, etc.)

Does your dog enjoy being with other dogs? If yes, how often is your dog around other dogs?

What types of cues will cause your dog to display anxiety? (i.e., pick- ing up the keys/putting on your coat)

Does your dog display the same level of separation anxiety symptoms if left in the morning versus being left in the evening?

Are there any types of absences your dog appears to not get anxious about? (i.e., taking out the garbage, leaving the house in slippers, etc.)

What amount of time would you like to be able to leave your dog alone in the future? (i.e., # of hours)

Have you done any behavioral work concerning your dog's separation anxiety before?

What does a typical 24-hour mid-week day entail for you and your dog?

What does a typical 24-hour weekend day entail for you and your dog?

Are you able to arrange your schedule to avoid leaving your dog alone for a few weeks or more?

Are you able to use a daycare, dog walker, dog sitter, or other service to keep your dog from having to experience absences for a while?

If you are currently using a dog walker, daycare, or other service to watch your dog, please provide their name:

Have you ever had a complaint from your neighbors regarding your dog's separation anxiety?

Will your neighbors (or landlord) affect your ability to work on your dog's separation anxiety? If yes, explain:

Who is your current veterinarian?

Have you spoken to your veterinarian about your dog's separation anxiety? If yes, did he/she make any recommendations?

If your dog's separation anxiety warrants pharmacological intervention, are you willing to discuss this with a veterinarian?

Is your dog sensitive to, fearful of, or anxious about noises?

If yes, list the types of noises that elicit a response from your dog:

Does your dog experience stress or anxiety during rain or thundershowers?

If yes, describe the behavior you observe during rain or thunder-showers:

Do you have any other behavioral concerns about your dog? If yes, please explain:

What type of food do you feed your dog? (List brands, quantities, etc.)

Does your dog take any supplements or vitamins?

What are your goals for this separation anxiety training?

Appendix 3
Sample Treatment Plans

Two treatment plans are provided in Appendix Three. Treatment Plan #1 is the basic treatment plan that most all clients will follow. Treatment Plan #2 is a basic treatment plan that includes the use of the Treat & Train.

Treatment Plan #1

Phase One

Preparation
- Review house layout and set up an area to be used for training.

- Read all articles and written materials to familiarize yourself with the plan.

- Begin teaching the new cues of GO-TO-MAT and STAY (review handout in Appendix One).

- Acquire baby gate, x-pen or crate, and interactive feeding toys.

Go-to-Mat criteria steps
1. Lure a GO-TO-MAT from right in front of the bed, rewarding each time. Repeat until you get five successful trials in a row.

2. Use verbal cue and hand signal to get GO-TO-MAT from right in front of the bed, rewarding each successful trial. Repeat until you get ten successful trials in a row.

3. Use verbal cue and hand signal to get GO-TO-MAT from one to two feet away, rewarding each successful trial. Repeat until you get ten successful trials in a row.

4. Use verbal cue and hand signal to get GO-TO-MAT from three to four feet away, rewarding each successful trial. Repeat until you get ten successful trials in a row.

RELAX/STAY criteria steps

Step 1:

If the criteria seem too high or too low in the below steps, adjust them accordingly. Unless directed otherwise you will stand in place facing your dog. Read through the steps once before you do them, so you understand the body directions. Note that this phase does not take place in the confinement area.

RELAX/STAY for two seconds, reward.

RELAX/STAY for four seconds, reward.

RELAX/STAY while you take one step back and return, reward.

RELAX/STAY while you take one step back and return, reward.

RELAX/STAY while you take one step back and return, reward.

RELAX/STAY for three seconds, reward.

RELAX/STAY while you take one step to the right and return, reward.

RELAX/STAY while you take one step to the left and return, reward.

RELAX/STAY for three seconds, reward.

RELAX/STAY while you take one step to the right and return, reward.

RELAX/STAY while you take one step to the left and return, reward.

RELAX/STAY for three seconds, reward.

RELAX/STAY while you take two steps back and return, reward.

RELAX/STAY for five seconds, reward.

RELAX/STAY while you turn your back and then turn right back around in place, reward.

RELAX/STAY for two seconds, reward.

RELAX/STAY while you clap your hands softly once, reward.

RELAX/STAY while you take three steps back and return, reward.

RELAX/STAY while you count out loud to five, reward.

RELAX/STAY while you clap your hands softly twice, reward.

RELAX/STAY while you count out loud to ten, reward.

RELAX/STAY while you turn your back and then turn back in place, reward.

RELAX/STAY while you clap your hands softly three times, reward.

RELAX/STAY for three seconds, reward.

RELAX/STAY while you turn your back take half a step forward and then turn back in place, reward.

RELAX/STAY for five seconds, reward.

RELAX/STAY for three seconds, reward.

Step 2:

RELAX/STAY for three seconds, reward.

RELAX/STAY for five seconds, reward.

RELAX/STAY while you take three steps back and return, reward.

RELAX/STAY while you turn your back and return, reward.

RELAX/STAY while you take five steps back and return, reward.

RELAX/STAY for two seconds, reward.

RELAX/STAY while you take three steps to the right and return, reward.

RELAX/STAY while you take three steps to the left and return, reward.

RELAX/STAY for three seconds, reward.

RELAX/STAY while you turn your back and take one step to the right and return, reward.

RELAX/STAY while you turn your back and take one step to the left and return, reward.

RELAX/STAY for seven seconds, reward.

RELAX/STAY for two seconds, reward.

RELAX/STAY while you turn your back and take three steps away (still in view) and return, reward.

RELAX/STAY for one second, reward.

RELAX/STAY for one second, reward.

RELAX/STAY for three seconds, reward.

RELAX/STAY for one second, reward.

RELAX/STAY while you turn your back and walk three steps away, return and reward.

RELAX/STAY for one second, reward.

RELAX/STAY while you turn your back for five seconds and turn back around, reward.

RELAX/STAY for two seconds, reward.

RELAX/STAY while you clap your hands softly twice, reward.

RELAX/STAY while you kneel to the ground on one knee briefly in place and stand back up, reward.

RELAX/STAY while you count out loud to five, reward.

RELAX/STAY while you clap your hands softly twice, reward.

RELAX/STAY while you walk just past your dog (behind him slightly) and back into place, reward.

RELAX/STAY for one second, reward.

RELAX/STAY for ten seconds, reward by tossing him a small jackpot of a few treats and end the session.

Step 3:
RELAX/STAY for three seconds, reward.

RELAX/STAY while you take five steps away and return, reward.

RELAX/STAY for three seconds, reward.

RELAX/STAY for seven seconds, reward.

RELAX/STAY while you walk into another room slightly out of view for one second and return, reward.

RELAX/STAY for two seconds, reward.

RELAX/STAY while you take three steps to the right and return, reward.

RELAX/STAY while you take three steps to the left and return, reward.

RELAX/STAY for twelve seconds, reward.

RELAX/STAY for three seconds, reward.

RELAX/STAY for one second, reward.

RELAX/STAY for three seconds, reward.

RELAX/STAY while you walk out of view for two seconds, return and reward.

RELAX/STAY for three seconds, reward.

RELAX/STAY while you to an interior closet, open and close it quickly, return and reward.

RELAX/STAY for seven seconds, reward.

RELAX/STAY for two seconds, reward.

RELAX/STAY while you walk out of view and count out loud for three seconds, return and reward.

RELAX/STAY for two seconds, reward.

RELAX/STAY for ten seconds, reward.

RELAX/STAY while you walk out of view for two seconds, return and reward.

RELAX/STAY for one second, reward.

RELAX/STAY for five seconds, reward.

RELAX/STAY while you turn your back for ten seconds and turn back around, reward.

RELAX/STAY for two seconds, reward.

RELAX/STAY while you do three jumping jacks, reward.

RELAX/STAY while you kneel to the ground on both knees briefly in place and stand back up, reward.

RELAX/STAY for two seconds, reward.

RELAX/STAY while you kneel to the ground on both knees for two seconds in place and stand back up, reward.

RELAX/STAY for ten seconds, reward.

RELAX/STAY while you clap your hands loudly twice, reward.

RELAX/STAY while you walk out of view and count out loud for five seconds, return and reward.

RELAX/STAY for five seconds, reward.

RELAX/STAY while you take three steps away and return, reward.

RELAX/STAY while you to an interior closet, open and close it quickly, return and reward.

RELAX/STAY while you take five steps away and return, reward.

RELAX/STAY for fifteen seconds, reward by tossing a small jackpot of a few treats and end the session.

Continue along these lines until you reach a RELAX/STAY of fifteen seconds from five feet away.

Later in the coming phases you will strengthen the STAY to one minute while out of view.

Phase Two

Preparation

- Build the GO-TO-MAT and RELAX/STAY up from beginning stages to 30 seconds and ten steps away.

- Install the baby gate or x-pen if using and begin in-view desensitization.

- Begin introducing interactive feeding devices and teach the game FIND IT.

In-view criteria steps

Note that these are sample steps and the criteria are written based on a dog with a moderate stress level. Adjust the steps to the specific dog, but keep the pace of the steps to ensure progress. Work on each step until the dog is able to handle the criteria level before you move on to the next step. Never push the dog to the point of anxiousness. On the other hand, if the dog is completely uninterested and calm, increase the difficulty

Step 1, all exits in view:

The dog must be settled and content at each level before you proceed to the next. If he isn't, stay at that level and repeat it until he is comfortable. Hang out after each return, so that each new exercise appears to be as close to a cold trial as possible. Vary the time increments, so each exit doesn't jump in time; mix it up with some longer and some shorter increments.

Step 1 can be broken into two phases:

- Begin by baiting the confinement area with the dog's favorite goodies. Allow him in and let him get into his food toys.

- Gradually step out and back in just standing alongside the baby gate. Allow the dog to settle before repeating this task. Spend plenty of time in the confinement area in between exiting.

- Repeat this task, increasing the time you spend outside the baby gate in increments of seconds at a time until you reach one minute.

- Vary the time increments so you have some shorter durations and some longer ones.

- If the dog shows any signs of stress, remain at that time level for a while until the dog is sufficiently desensitized to that plateau. Only then move on to the next task.

In the second phase, begin in the confinement area:

- Give the dog his interactive feeding toy and let him start to eat. Walk nonchalantly out of the baby-gated area (while staying in view) and return after one minute. Pause for 20 to 30 seconds while the dog settles so that each new exercise is as close to a cold trial as possible.

- Repeat this task, increasing the time you spend outside the confinement area in increments of seconds and then minutes at a time until you reach a duration of 30 minutes.

- Vary the time increments so you have some shorter durations and some longer ones.
- If the dog shows any signs of stress, stay at that level until the dog is sufficiently desensitized to that plateau. Only then move on to the next task.
- Make sure that during this time the dog learns to run out of food in the interactive feeding toy and remain settled without it.

The dog should be relaxed and unfazed by the above absences before you proceed to the next step. This process is relatively quick for most dogs. If a dog is having difficulty, reward him for any increment of calm behavior in the confinement area to build duration.

Step 2, exits are in partially obstructed view:

Begin in the confinement area:

- Give the dog his interactive feeding toy and let him start to eat. Walk nonchalantly out of the baby-gated area into an area partly obstructed from view, for example behind a kitchen counter or halfway into the threshold of a doorway. Return immediately and pause for 20 to 30 seconds while the dog settles so that each new exercise is as close to a cold trial as possible.
- Build duration in increments of minutes up to 30 minutes outside the confinement area while you stand in view but partially obstructed. Make sure you pause long enough between exits.
- Vary the time increments so you have some shorter durations and some longer ones.
- If the dog shows any signs of stress, stay at that level until the dog is sufficiently desensitized to that plateau. Only then move on to the next task.
- Make sure that during this time the dog runs out of food in the interactive feeding toy and can remain settled without it. Reward for calm if the dog is having difficulty with this task and make certain you fully desensitize the dog before you move on to the next task.

Phase Three

Preparation

- Use the GO-TO-MAT and RELAX/STAY cues as part of the non-follow routine regularly.

- Begin desensitization to out-of-view absences.

- Use interactive feeding devices and the game FIND IT for feeding in confinement area.

- Watch video to help determine baseline for future criteria setting.

Out-of-view criteria steps

Begin in the confinement area.

- Give the dog his interactive feeding toy and let him start to eat. Walk nonchalantly out of the baby-gated area, go to an area entirely out of view, and return immediately. Pause for 20 to 30 seconds, allowing the dog to settle so that each new exercise is as close to a cold trial as possible.

- Repeat this task, increasing in increments of seconds then minutes until you reach 30 minutes. Make sure you pause long enough between each exit.

- Vary the time increments so you have some shorter durations and some longer ones.

- If the dog shows any signs of stress, stay at that level until the dog is sufficiently desensitized to that plateau. Only then move on to the next task.

- Make sure that during this time if the dog runs out of food in the interactive feeding toy he can remain settled without it. Reward for calm if the dog is having difficulty with this task and make certain you fully desensitize the dog before you move on to the next task. (The Treat & Train can help significantly with out-of-view absences.)

Do the following steps once the dog has been fully desensitized to a 30-minute out-of-view absence in his confinement area both with and without food. Mix up the steps once you have accomplished some of the easier ones.

- Walk nonchalantly out of the baby-gated area and walk half-way to the front door while carrying your keys, and return.

Pause for 20 to 30 seconds, allowing the dog to settle completely so that each new exercise is as close to a cold trial as possible. Repeat the task until the dog is entirely uninterested.

- Walk nonchalantly out of the baby-gated area and walk all the way to the front door without touching it while carrying your keys, and return. Pause for 20 to 30 seconds, allowing the dog to settle so that each new exercise is as close to a cold trial as possible. Repeat the task until the dog is entirely uninterested.

- Walk nonchalantly out of the baby-gated area and walk all the way to the front door and touch the door, but not the door knob, while carrying your keys. Pause for 20 to 30 seconds, allowing the dog to settle so that each new exercise is as much like a cold trial as possible. Repeat the task until the dog is entirely uninterested.

- Walk nonchalantly out of the baby-gated area and walk all the way to the front door, touch the doorknob, still carrying your keys, and return. Pause for 20 to 30 seconds, allowing the dog to settle so that each new exercise is as close to a cold trial as possible. Repeat the task until the dog is entirely uninterested.

- Walk out of the baby-gated area and walk to the front door. Crack the front door open slightly, close it, and return immediately. Pause for 20 to 30 seconds, allowing the dog to settle so that each new exercise is as close to a cold trial as possible. Repeat the task until the dog is entirely uninterested.

- Walk out of the baby-gated area to the front door. Open the front door halfway and close it, returning immediately. Pause for 20 to 30 seconds, allowing the dog to settle so that each new exercise is as close to a cold trial as possible. Repeat the task until the dog is entirely uninterested.

- Walk out of the baby-gated area to the front door. Open the front door all the way, close it, and return immediately. Pause for 20 to 30 seconds, allowing the dog to settle so that each new exercise is as close to a cold trial as possible. Repeat the task until the dog is entirely uninterested.

By the end of this phase, you should be able to open and close the front door about 15 to 20 times in the span of 30 minutes without getting any stressed reaction from the dog.

Phase Four

Preparation

- Use the GO-TO-MAT and RELAX/STAY cues as part of the non-follow routine regularly.

- Begin desensitization plan to walk out of the front door (see criteria steps).

- Watch video regularly to help assess and determine criteria setting.

Front door criteria steps

Begin your session by warming up the dog with a few open-and-close-door exercises.

- Exit the baby-gated area. Walk to the front door, open and close the front door, and return, allowing the dog to settle so that each new exercise is as close to a cold trial as possible. Repeat several times.

- Exit the baby-gated area. Walk to the front door, open the door, step out and immediately back in, close the door and return, allowing the dog to settle so that each new exercise is as close to a cold trial as possible. Repeat until the dog is unconcerned by the process.

- Exit the baby-gated area. Walk to the front door, open the door, step out for the duration of one second, close the door and return, allowing the dog to settle so that each new exercise is as close to a cold trial as possible. Repeat at least ten times or until the dog is unconcerned by the process.

- Using remote video, watch the dog during absences and begin to increase duration in increments of seconds up to ten seconds. Use a variable ratio: sometimes longer durations, sometimes shorter. Repeat these rehearsals until the dog is completely unconcerned about the activity.

- Once you reach a duration of about ten seconds, switch to simply dead-bolting the front door and immediately returning (if you use a dead bolt). Repeat until the dog is completely uninterested by the activity.

- Using remote video, watch the dog during absences with the door locked and begin to increase duration in increments of seconds until you reach one minute. Use a variable ratio:

sometimes longer durations, sometimes shorter. Repeat until the dog is completely uninterested by the activity.

- Once you reach a duration of one minute, you can jump time increments in larger segments of ten to twenty seconds. Use video to carefully monitor the dog's body language.

- Once you achieve a fifteen-minute absence and the dog's body language shows the absence is successful, you can jump time increments in larger segments of 20 to 60 seconds. Again, use video to carefully monitor the dog's body language.

Build absence duration to 30 minutes or more, and make certain you incorporate all of the elements of a typical departure, such as garage doors or main apartment building doors. Also incorporate cues that may be significant, for example bringing a bag with you.

Phase Five

Preparation
- Use the GO-TO-MAT and RELAX/STAY cues as part of the non-follow routine regularly.

- Build on desensitization plan to increase duration absences through to maintenance.

- Use interactive feeding devices and FIND IT for feeding including during maintenance.

- Watch video regularly to help assess and determine criteria setting.

Duration build-up criteria steps
At this point, you are able to use the game of FIND IT when you leave, as well as other interactive feeding toys. Building on the 30-minute duration from Phase Four, absences will continue to gradually increase in increments of minutes up to four hours. Once you have built duration sufficiently, you can jump by increases of five minutes or more, but do use video monitoring to pay careful attention to body language.

Duration build-up will typically look something like this:

- Thirty minutes to one hour: Build in increments of three- to five-minute chunks.

- One to two hours: Build in increments of five- to fifteen-minute chunks.

- Two to four hours: Build in increments of fifteen- to thirty-minute chunks.

Maintenance can begin once you reach absences of two hours or more. Often, you can carry out absence maintenance at this level to ensure continued success without having to constantly vary the time intervals dramatically. I do suggest that you desensitize the dog fully to durations of up to four hours, if that's your desired time frame in the future. I have found that, for most dogs, it's an easy task to fade out the baby gate, and even the crate if one was used. But this must be done weeks or months down the line after the dog has had considerable success rehearsing the full length of an owner absence. When you fade out the confinement apparatus, all you need to do initially is leave it open. In time, you can completely disassemble it. If you see any regression when the gate is left open, then do some basic desensitization exercises with shorter durations or by adding additional feeding toys to the mix. Fortunately, regression here is fairly rare. Remember, it's not *necessary* to fade out the baby gate or the crate. It's an option, not a requirement.

Treatment Plan #2

Using the Treat & Train

Phase One
Preparation

- Review the house layout and set up an area to be used for training.
- Read all articles and written materials to familiarize yourself with the plan.
- Begin teaching the new cues of GO-TO-MAT and RELAX/ STAY (review handout in Appendix 3).
- Acquire baby gate, x-pen or crate and interactive feeding toys, including the Treat & Train.

MAT criteria steps
1. Lure a GO-TO-MAT from right in front of the bed, rewarding each time. Repeat until you get five successful trials.

2. Use verbal cue and hand signal to get GO-TO-MAT from right in front of the bed. rewarding each successful trial. Repeat until you get ten successful trials.

3. Use verbal cue and hand signal to get GO-TO-MAT from one and two feet away, rewarding each successful trial. Repeat until you get ten successful trials.

4. Use verbal cue and hand signal to get GO-TO-MAT from three and four feet away, rewarding each successful trial. Repeat until you get ten successful trials.

RELAX/STAY criteria steps

Step 1:
If the criteria seem too high or too low in these steps, adjusted them accordingly. Unless directed otherwise, you will stand in place while *facing* your dog. Read through the steps once before you do them, so you understand the body directions.

RELAX/STAY for two seconds, reward.

RELAX/STAY for four seconds, reward.

RELAX/STAY while you take one step back and return, reward.

RELAX/STAY while you take one step back and return, reward.

RELAX/STAY while you take one step back and return, reward.

RELAX/STAY for three seconds, reward.

RELAX/STAY while you take one step to the right and return, reward.

RELAX/STAY while you take one step to the left and return, reward.

RELAX/STAY for three seconds, reward.

RELAX/STAY while you take one step to the right and return, reward.

RELAX/STAY while you take one step to the left and return, reward.

RELAX/STAY for three seconds, reward.

RELAX/STAY while you take two steps back and return, reward.

RELAX/STAY for five seconds, reward.

RELAX/STAY while you turn your back and then turn right back around in place, reward.

RELAX/STAY for two seconds, reward.

RELAX/STAY while you clap your hands softly once, reward.

RELAX/STAY while you take three steps back and return, reward.

RELAX/STAY while you count out loud to five, reward.

RELAX/STAY while you clap your hands softly twice, reward.

RELAX/STAY while you count out loud to ten, reward.

RELAX/STAY while you turn your back and then turn back in place, reward.

RELAX/STAY while you clap your hands softly three times, reward.

RELAX/STAY for three seconds, reward.

RELAX/STAY while you turn your back take half a step forward and then turn back in place, reward.

RELAX/STAY for five seconds, reward.

RELAX/STAY for three seconds, reward.

Step 2:

RELAX/STAY for three seconds, reward.

RELAX/STAY for five seconds, reward.

RELAX/STAY while you take three steps back and return, reward.

RELAX/STAY while you turn your back and return, reward.

RELAX/STAY while you take five steps back and return, reward.

RELAX/STAY for two seconds, reward.

RELAX/STAY while you take three steps to the right and return, reward.

RELAX/STAY while you take three steps to the left and return, reward.

RELAX/STAY for three seconds, reward.

RELAX/STAY while you turn your back and take one step to the right and return, reward.

RELAX/STAY while you turn your back and take one step to the left and return, reward.

RELAX/STAY for seven seconds, reward.

RELAX/STAY for two seconds, reward.

RELAX/STAY while you turn your back and take three steps away (still in view) and return, reward.

RELAX/STAY for one second, reward.

RELAX/STAY for one second, reward.

RELAX/STAY for three seconds, reward.

RELAX/STAY for one second, reward.

RELAX/STAY while you turn your back and walk three steps away, return and reward.

RELAX/STAY for one second, reward.

RELAX/STAY while you turn your back for five seconds and turn back around, reward.

RELAX/STAY for two seconds, reward.

RELAX/STAY while you clap your hands softly twice, reward.

RELAX/STAY while you kneel to the ground on one knee briefly in place and stand back up, reward.

RELAX/STAY while you count out loud to five, reward.

RELAX/STAY while you clap your hands softly twice, reward.

RELAX/STAY while you walk just past your dog (behind him slightly) and back into place, reward.

RELAX/STAY for one second, reward.

RELAX/STAY for ten seconds, reward by tossing him a jackpot of a few treats and end the session.

Step 3:

RELAX/STAY for three seconds, reward.

RELAX/STAY while you take five steps away and return, reward.

RELAX/STAY for three seconds, reward.

RELAX/STAY for seven seconds, reward.

RELAX/STAY while you walk into another room slightly out of view for one second and return, reward.

RELAX/STAY for two seconds, reward.

RELAX/STAY while you take three steps to the right and return, reward.

RELAX/STAY while you take three steps to the left and return, reward.

RELAX/STAY for twelve seconds, reward.

RELAX/STAY for three seconds, reward.

RELAX/STAY for one second, reward.

RELAX/STAY for three seconds, reward.

RELAX/STAY while you walk out of view for two seconds, return and reward.

RELAX/STAY for three seconds, reward.

RELAX/STAY while you walk to an interior closet, open and close it quickly, and return, reward.

RELAX/STAY for seven seconds, reward.

RELAX/STAY for two seconds, reward.

RELAX/STAY while you walk out of view and count out loud for three seconds, return and reward.

RELAX/STAY for two seconds, reward.

RELAX/STAY for ten seconds, reward.

RELAX/STAY while you walk out of view for two seconds, return and reward.

RELAX/STAY for one second, reward.

RELAX/STAY for five seconds, reward.

RELAX/STAY while you turn your back for ten seconds and turn back around, reward.

RELAX/STAY for two seconds, reward.

RELAX/STAY while you do three jumping jacks, reward.

RELAX/STAY while you kneel to the ground on both knees briefly in place and stand back up, reward.

RELAX/STAY for two seconds, reward.

RELAX/STAY while you kneel to the ground on both knees for two seconds in place and stand back up, reward.

RELAX/STAY for ten seconds, reward.

RELAX/STAY while you clap your hands loudly twice, reward.

RELAX/STAY while you walk out of view and count out loud for five seconds, return and reward.

RELAX/STAY for five seconds, reward.

RELAX/STAY while you take three steps away and return, reward.

RELAX/STAY while you walk to an interior closet, open and close it quickly, return and reward.

RELAX/STAY while you take five steps away and return, reward.

RELAX/STAY for fifteen seconds, reward by tossing a jackpot of a few treats and end the session.

Continue along these lines until you reach a RELAX/STAY of fifteen seconds from five feet away.

Later in the coming phases you will strengthen the STAY to one minute while out of view.

Phase Two

Preparation

- Build the MAT and RELAX/STAY up from beginning stages to 30 seconds and ten steps away

- Introduce and desensitize the Treat & Train

- Install the baby gate or x-pen if using and begin in-view desensitization

Introducing the Treat & Train

This is where you introduce the Treat & Train in your program. You can review the process of desensitizing the dog to the turnstile on page 43.

In-view criteria steps

These are sample steps and the criteria are written based on a dog with a moderate stress level. Adjust the steps to the specific dog, but keep the pace of the steps to ensure progress. Work on each step until the dog is able to handle the criteria level before you move on to the next step. Never push the dog to the point of anxiousness. On the other hand, if the dog is completely uninterested, increase the difficulty.

Step 1, all exits in view:

The dog must be settled and content at each level before you proceed to the next. If he isn't, stay at that level and repeat it until he is comfortable. Hang out after each return so that each new exercise appears to be as close to a cold trial as possible. Vary the time increments, so each exit doesn't jump in time; mix it up with some longer and some shorter increments.

Step 1 can be broken into two phases:

- Begin by placing the Treat & Train in the confinement area and have the dog lie down in front of it. Using the remote control, dispense from the Treat & Train a few times to keep the dog engaged.

- Gradually step out and back in, standing right by the baby gate—dispense most heavily when you are stepping out of the gate. Allow the dog to settle before you repeat this task. Spend plenty of time in the confinement area in between exits.

- Repeat this task, increasing in increments of seconds at a time until you reach one minute.

- Vary the time increments so you have some shorter durations and some longer ones.

- If the dog shows any signs of stress, stay at that time level until the dog is sufficiently desensitized to that plateau. Only then move on to the next task.

In the second phase, begin in the confinement area:

- Dispense a few times before you exit, but dispense most heavily while you are out of the confinement area. Walk nonchalantly out of the baby-gated area while staying in view, and return in one minute. Pause for 20 to 30 seconds, allowing time for the dog to settle so that each new exercise is as close to a cold trial as possible.

- Once you reach a duration of about two or three minutes, you can switch from using the remote control to the automated dispense mode. For most dogs, starting at the 20-second ratio is comfortable, but if that's too difficult for the dog, drop it to 10.

- Repeat the task of exiting and entering, increasing in increments of seconds and then minutes at a time until you reach a 30-minute duration. Leave the Treat & Train in the 20-second dispense mode for now.

- Vary the time increments so you have some shorter durations and some longer ones.

- If the dog shows any signs of stress, stay at that level for a while until the dog is sufficiently desensitized to that plateau. Only then move on to the next task.

- Using the remote control, turn off the Treat & Train for increments of a minute at a time toward the end of the session to allow the dog to have brief periods without the food dispensing.

- Once the dog is comfortable with a 30-minute absence at the 20-second dispense mode, raise the time dispense ratio on the Treat & Train to 30 seconds.

The dog should be relaxed and unfazed by the above absences before you proceed to the next step. This process is relatively quick for most dogs.

Step 2, exits are in partially obstructed view:
Begin in the confinement area:

- Activate the Treat & Train, which should now be set at the 30-second dispense ratio. Walk nonchalantly out of the baby-gated area into an area partly obstructed from view, such as behind a kitchen counter or partially into a threshold of a doorway. Return immediately and pause for 20 to 30 seconds, allowing the dog to settle before the next exercise so that each exercise is as close to a cold trial as possible.

- Once the dog is comfortable with approximately fifteen minutes of partially obstructed-view absences, increase the dispense ratio on the Treat & Train to 45 seconds.

- Build duration in increments of minutes until you can spend 30 minutes outside the confinement area while in partially obstructed view. Make sure you pause long enough between exits.

- Vary the time increments so you have some shorter durations and some longer ones.

- If the dog shows any signs of stress, stay at that level for a while until the dog is sufficiently desensitized to that plateau. Only then move on to the next task.

- Using the remote control, turn off the Treat & Train for two minutes at a time toward the end of the session to let the dog to experience brief periods without the food dispensing.

Phase Three

Preparation
- Use the GO-TO-MAT and STAY cues as part of the non-follow routine regularly.

- Begin desensitization plan to out-of-view absences.

- Watch video to help determine baseline for future criteria setting.

Out-of-view criteria steps

- Begin in the confinement area. Activate the Treat & Train, which should now be set at 45 seconds. Have the remote control with you in the event you need to reward more frequently when stepping out of view. Walk nonchalantly out of the baby-gated area and go to an area entirely out of view and return immediately. Pause for 20 to 30 seconds to allow the dog to settle before you repeat this task so that each exercise is as close to a cold trial as possible.

- Once the dog is successfully handling fifteen minutes of out-of-view absences, raise the dispense rate on the Treat & Train to 60 seconds.

- Repeat the out-of-view absences, increasing in increments of seconds then minutes until you reach a duration of 30 minutes. Make sure you pause long enough between each exit.

- Vary the time increments so you have some shorter durations and some longer ones.

- If the dog shows any signs of stress, stay at that level until the dog is sufficiently desensitized to that plateau. Only then move on to the next task.

- Using the remote control, turn off the Treat & Train for increments of three minutes at a time toward the end of the session to let the dog experience brief periods without the food dispensing.

You will do the below steps once you have fully desensitized the dog to a 30-minute out-of-view absence in his confinement area. Mix up the steps once you accomplish some of the easier ones. Take the remote control with you so you can dispense most heavily at the hardest point of the task when needed.

- Walk nonchalantly out of the baby-gated area and walk halfway to the front door while carrying your keys, and return. Pause for 20 to 30 seconds, allowing the dog to settle so that each new exercise is as close to a cold trial as possible. Repeat this task until the dog is completely uninterested.

- Walk nonchalantly out of the baby-gated area and walk all the way to the front door without touching it while carrying your keys, and return. Pause for 20 to 30 seconds, allowing the dog to settle so that each new exercise is as close to a cold trial as possible. Repeat until the dog is completely uninterested.

- Walk nonchalantly out of the baby-gated area and walk all the way to the front door and touch the door but not the door knob while carrying your keys, and return. Pause for 20 to 30 seconds, allowing the dog to settle so that each new exercise is as close to a cold trial as possible. Repeat until the dog is completely uninterested.

- Walk nonchalantly out of the baby-gated area and walk all the way to the front door, touch the doorknob, still carrying your keys, and return. Pause for 20 to 30 seconds, allowing the dog to settle so that each new exercise is as close to a cold trial as possible. Repeat until the dog is completely uninterested.

- Walk out of the baby-gated area and walk to the front door. Crack the front door open slightly, close it, and return immediately. Pause for 20 to 30 seconds, allowing the dog to settle so that each new exercise is as close to a cold trial as possible. Repeat until the dog is completely uninterested.

- Walk out of the baby-gated area to the front door. Open the front door halfway and close it, returning immediately. Pause for 20 to 30 seconds, allowing the dog to settle so that each new exercise is as close to a cold trial as possible. Repeat until the dog is completely uninterested.

- Walk out of the baby-gated area to the front door. Open the front door all the way, close it, and return immediately. Pause for 20 to 30 seconds, allowing the dog to settle so that each new exercise is as close to a cold trial as possible. Repeat until the dog is completely uninterested.

By the end of this phase, you should be able to open and close the front door about ten to fifteen times in the span of 30 minutes without getting any stressful reaction from the dog. The Treat & Train will be running throughout the session at the 60 second rate of reinforcement.

Phase Four

Preparation

- Use the GO-TO-MAT and RELAX/STAY cues as part of the non-follow routine regularly.

- Begin desensitization plan to walk out of the front door (see criteria steps).

- Watch video regularly to help assess and determine criteria setting

Front door exercises

Begin your session by warming up the dog with a few open-and-close-door exercises. The Treat & Train should still be set at 60 seconds.

- Exit the baby-gated area. Walk to the front door, open and close the front door, and return, allowing the dog to settle before you repeat the task. Repeat several times.

- Exit the baby-gated area. Walk to the front door, open the door, step out and immediately back in, close the door and return allowing the dog to settle so that each new exercise is as close to a cold trial as possible. Repeat the above until the dog is unconcerned by the process

- Exit the baby-gated area. Walk to the front door, open the door, step out for the duration of one second, close the door, and return, allowing the dog to settle so that each new exercise is as close to a cold trial as possible. Repeat at least ten times or until the dog is unconcerned by the process

- Using remote video, watch the dog during absences and begin to increase duration in increments of seconds up to ten seconds. Use a variable ratio: sometimes longer durations, sometimes shorter. Repeat these rehearsals until the dog is completely unconcerned about the activity.

- Once you reach a duration of about ten seconds, switch to simply dead-bolting the front door, and immediately returning (if you use a dead bolt). Repeat until the dog is completely uninterested by this activity.

- Using remote video, watch the dog during absences with the door locked and begin to increase duration in increments of seconds up to one minute. Use a variable ratio: sometimes longer durations, sometimes shorter. Repeat until the dog is completely uninterested by the activity.

- Once you reach a duration of one minute, you can jump time increments in larger segments of ten to twenty seconds. Use video monitoring to pay careful attention to body language.

- Once you achieve a fifteen-minute absence and the dog's body language shows the absence is successful, you can jump time increments can be jumped in larger segments of 20 to 30 seconds. Use video monitoring to pay careful attention to body language.

- Build absence duration to 30 minutes or more, and make certain you incorporate all of the elements of a typical departure, such as garage doors or main apartment building doors. Also incorporate cues that may be significant, for example bringing a bag with you.

Once you reach 30-minute absences and all exit protocols have been included, you can raise the dispense ratio on the Treat & Train to 120 seconds. Do watch the dog carefully via video when you do this, as this is a big jump.

Phase Five

Preparation

- Use the GO-TO-MAT and RELAX/STAY cues as part of the non-follow routine regularly.

- Build on desensitization plan to increase duration absences through to maintenance.

- Watch video regularly to help assess and determine criteria setting.

Criteria steps for duration build-up

At this point, the Treat & Train has been raised to 120 seconds and the dog is comfortably handling a 30-minute absence. Building on the 30-minute duration from Phase Four, continue to gradually increase absences in increments of minutes through to four hours. Once you have built enough duration, you can jump in increments of five minutes or more, but do pay careful attention to body language, preferably by monitoring video closely. Typically, the Treat & Train can be raised to a dispense rate of 300 seconds around the one-hour mark.

You can begin maintenance once you reach absences of two hours or more. Often, you can practice maintaining absences at this level to ensure continued success without having to constantly vary the time intervals dramatically. I do suggest you fully desensitize the dog to durations up to four hours if that's the desired time frame for the future.

Duration build-up will typically look like this:

- Thirty minutes to one hour: Build in increments of three- to five-minute chunks.

- One to two hours: Build in increments of five- to fifteen-minute chunks.

- Two to four hours: Build in increments of fifteen- to thirty-minute chunks.

Around the two-hour point, it's important to teach the dog that it's no emergency if the Treat & Train runs out or is turned off. Using the remote control, turn off the Treat & Train from outside about ten to fifteen minutes before you return. Build that up to half an hour and eventually to longer still. This is rarely a problem for dogs, but I do think it's an important step, just in case the Treat & Train runs out of food, gets jammed, or runs out of battery.

Appendix 4
Recommended Reading
and Viewing

Recommended Client Reading:
Don't Shoot the Dog by Karen Pryor

Canine Behavior; A Photo Illustrated Handbook by Barbara Handelman

Canine Body Language by Brenda Aloff

Plenty in Life is Free by Kathy Sdao

The Culture Clash by Jean Donaldson

On Talking Terms with Dogs by Turid Rugaas

Recommended Video Links to View:
One Year old dog, Weston – in his crate displaying very typical signs of separation anxiety
https://www.youtube.com/watch?v=1MzjRfGdhJs

Puppy Leo the Husky mix displaying very typical separation anxiety vocalization
https://www.youtube.com/watch?v=agnOSMS_4o0

Border Collie with separation anxiety bites on crate bars and vocalizes
https://www.youtube.com/watch?v=TE6Vpm1U7LM

Dog loose in house with separation anxiety shows great stress cues while left alone
http://www.youtube.com/watch?v=YB90JNhVKt8

Dog loose in house displaying some mild to moderate destruction
http://www.youtube.com/watch?v=oX8QqvWV3vA

Boston Terrier Puppy with anxiety
http://www.youtube.com/watch?v=jFjl7grzJ1c

For information on participating in the online Separation Anxiety Internship Program, please got to www.malenademartini.com

For a Webinar presentation about this information please see the past recordings at www.petprofessionalguild.com or go to the following link:

http://www.petprofessionalguild.com/GuildTrainingWebinars?eventId=830238&EventViewMode=EventDetails

About the Author

Malena DeMartini-Price, CTC, is a San Francisco SPCA Academy for Dog Trainers honors graduate with over 13 years experience. In that time she has worked with several hundred separation anxiety cases. As a trainer who exclusively handles separation anxiety in her practice, she has found numerous creative solutions for a disorder that often baffles owners and trainers alike.

Her particular strength lies in reading the subtleties of dog body language and guiding owners patiently and with great enthusiasm through the gentle process of healing their dogs. Using web technology, Malena counsels clients all over the country and even a few international clients, giving her an unusually keen view of different types of scenarios.

Malena has written for APDT's *Chronicle of the Dog* and has given her seminar *Fixing the Unfixable* nationwide. She recently spoke at the 20th Anniversary APDT Conference and has presented numerous Webinars including ones for Jean Donaldson's Academy for Dog Trainers and the Pet Professional Guild. She is also now starting an online internship program for trainers to help them learn the detailed process of treating separation anxiety.

Malena's practice is located in Sonoma County, CA where she lives with her husband Kevin, also a certified trainer, her two rescue dogs, Leia and Tini, and a myriad of visiting separation anxiety dog friends that hang out here and there while completing their training.

Gina Phairas, Bsc Comms, CTC, helps trainers succeed across the country as a business consultant and leading force behind dog*tec. Gina brings her marketing and communications background to her work with dog professionals, as well as her extensive training resume. She is a former San Francisco SPCA Academy for Dog Trainers instructor, and as the SF/SPCA Rehabilitation Coordinator developed and oversaw staff training. Gina speaks regularly on business topics at conferences and seminars across the country.

Index

Also available from Dogwise Publishing

Go to www.dogwise.com for more books and ebooks.

Do Over Dogs
Give Your Dog a Second Chance for a First Class Life
Pat Miller

What exactly is a Do-Over Dog? It might be a shelter dog you're working with to help her become more adoptable. Perhaps it's the dog you've adopted, rescued, or even found running stray who is now yours to live with and love...forever. Or it could be the dog you've lived with for years but you realize he still has "issues" that make him a challenging canine companion. A Do-Over Dog is any dog that you think needs—make that deserves—a second chance in life.

The Human Half of Dog Training
Collaborating with Clients to Get Results
Risë VanFleet

One challenge for many trainers is that their success with dogs ultimately depends on the cooperation, understanding and follow-through of the people whose dogs are being trained. In The Human Half of Dog Training, author Risë VanFleet draws upon her experience as a child and family psychologist to teach dog trainers how to take a collaborative approach with clients to help insure the best possible outcomes for their dogs.

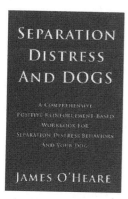

Separation Distress and Dogs
James O'Heare

Separation Distress and Dogs is a positive reinforcement based workbook for understanding, assessing and changing separation distress related behaviors in dogs. Written for guardians of dogs who exhibit distress behaviors when left alone, it presents an easy to follow, yet comprehensive, behavior change program. Includes systematic desensitization and behavior shaping, as well as empowerment training and relationship rehabilitation. It also includes sections for professional behavior consultants.

Canine Body Language
A Photographic Guide
Brenda Aloff

Canine Body Language by Brenda Aloff is a guide to canine body language. Never before has the body language of dogs been so thoroughly documented with photographs and text. Hundreds of images in this almost 400 page book illustrate the incredible variety of postures, behaviors and situations that the typical dog either manifests or encounters in his day-to-day life.

Dogwise.com is your source for quality books, ebooks, DVDs, training tools and treats.

We've been selling to the dog fancier for more than 25 years and we carefully screen our products for quality information, safety, durability and FUN! You'll find something for every level of dog enthusiast on our website www.dogwise.com or drop by our store in Wenatchee, Washington.

68041127R00108

Made in the USA
Middletown, DE
27 March 2018